New Horizons

05

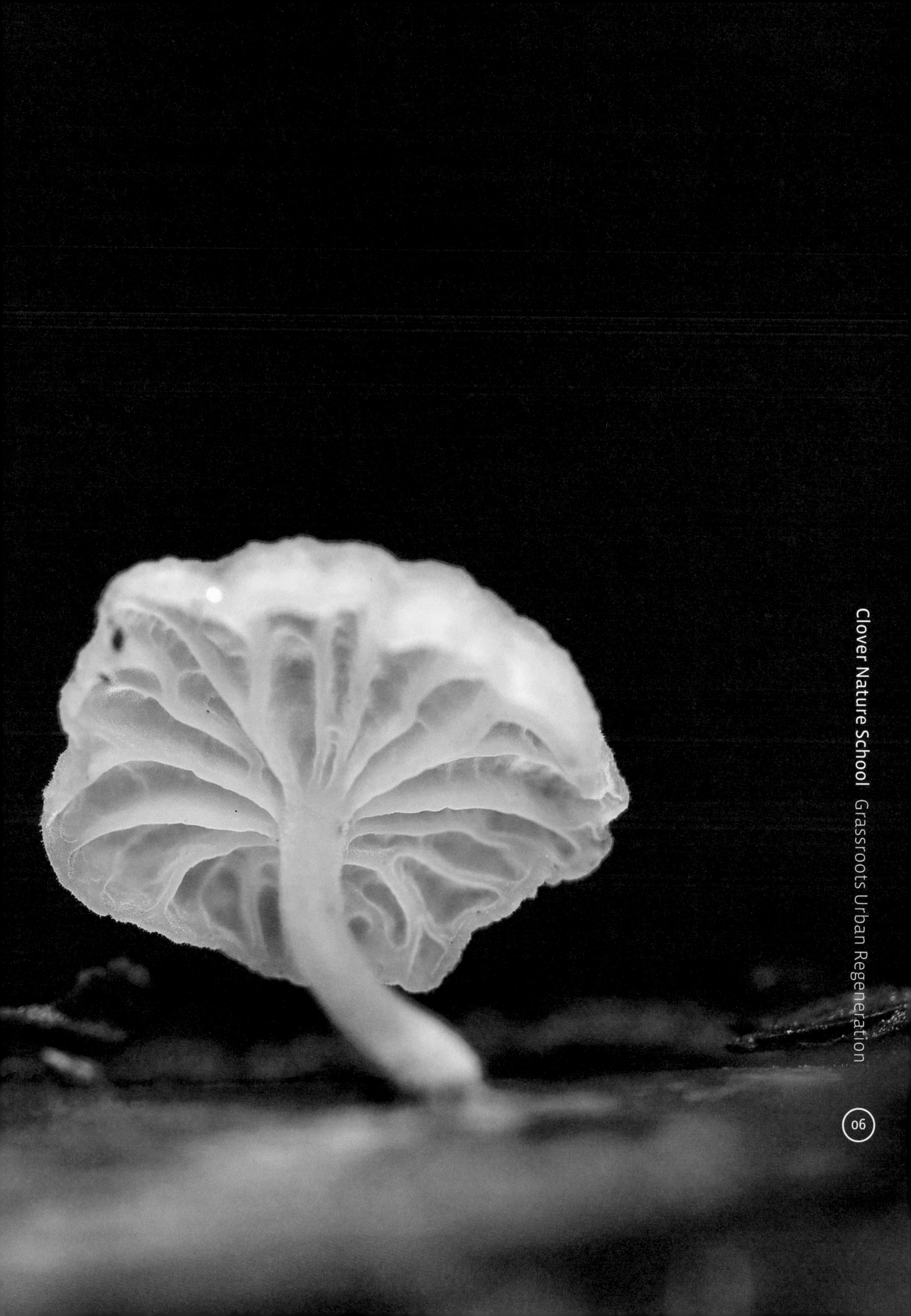

lab D+H Landscapes of Optimism

08

New Horizons

Eight Perspectives on Chinese Landscape Architecture Today

Jutta Kehrer (Ed.)

Birkhäuser
Basel

Foreword

Since the mid-1990s, when Western architects began heading to China in search of opportunities to make their mark in seemingly uncharted architectural territory, Aedes has been raising the opposite question: "What comes from China? What is the status of contemporary Chinese architecture?" The exhibition TU-MU at the Aedes Architecture Forum in 2001, which for the first time presented independent Chinese architecture studios to an international audience outside of China, was an early and groundbreaking result of these initial questions. In the years that followed, my partner and co-director Hans-Jürgen Commerell and I became ambassadors of dialogue and exchange between the Chinese architecture avant-garde and Europe. The many encounters, trustful collaborations and intense debates we were rewarded with during the past two decades of our China involvement remain an exceptional experience.

When Jutta Kehrer approached me regarding the preface of this inspiring publication, I immediately agreed, as I could clearly sense the similarity of experience and excitement in observing a contemporary avant-garde in Chinese landscape architecture today.

In 2002, when I was a jury member of the international masterplanning competition for the Olympic Green in Beijing, I realised how most of the international submissions failed in providing a deeper understanding of the cultural connotations of such an iconic civic venue, as the Olympic Park would be for Beijing. Years later, by contrast, the ease by which this new generation of Chinese landscape architects combine Chinese landscape traditions and sensitivities with a modern international design expression is exceptional and astounding at the same time. This publication definitely opens up *New Horizons* by showing projects that push the boundaries – from poetic to spectacular – from high-density urban quarters to the peripheries and China's rural hinterland.

The featured projects also demonstrate a new thinking apparent in the design field across disciplines in China. The focus in architecture has shifted away from commercial projects to cultural institutions, from museums to libraries and educational establishments. Equally, the emphasis in urban development has turned from city expansion to inner-city renewal on both the macro- and microscale. With growing prosperity, societal demands on public urban spaces are changing. Placemaking and user-centred design are gaining momentum in inner cities and becoming the driver for urban renewal projects advocating inclusiveness and liveability.

The wide range of projects and topics presented in this book has not only the potential to spark the rethinking of the relationship between both architecture and landscape architecture, and the city and the rural, but also to stimulate the dialogue between Asia and the Western hemisphere in a continuously changing and challenging world.

Kristin Feireiss

Editor's note:
Throughout the book, the Chinese proper names are given in the traditional order, with surnames first.

New Horizons

Introduction

China's New Landscape Architecture Avant-garde

Innovative, Optimistic, Radical yet Rooted

Jutta Kehrer

It is happening. China's landscape architecture profession is changing. A new avant-garde of independent Chinese landscape architecture studios is on the rise. They offer a refreshed view of Chinese landscape architecture practice and design thinking from within. They promote progress as well as critical reflection. Eight prominent studios are portrayed in this book. They take a stance on high-density urban living, sustainable renewal and user participation from the booming cities on China's eastern coast to the remote rural hinterland. Their founders are the thought leaders and influencers of an entire generation of young landscape architects in China.

The featured studios are the forerunners of a new chapter in Chinese landscape architecture practice. Moderate in size and led by their founders as Design Principals, they counterbalance the established portfolio of large-scale Local Design Institutes (LDIs) and international design and engineering companies. The selection of studios represents a spectrum of new voices in landscape architecture including well-known landscape architecture firms WISTO and Z+T Studio, newcomers Instinct Fabrication, lab D+H and YIYU, Moshang, a new specialist practice, and studios concerned with participatory design such as Clover Nature School and Fu Yingbin Studio. Their projects address topics ranging from community gardens to urban farming, from Chinese traditions and art history to applications of new technologies and from micro-regeneration of old city quarters to sustainable landscapes in China's new eco-towns.

With the diversity of new leaders in landscape architecture came innovation, exchange and debate. The landscape architecture profession in China is discussing more extensively than ever. The avant-garde of new studios has accelerated not only market dynamics but the vibe and creative spirit of the entire industry. The interviews and featured projects provide insight into the current discourse in China and raise questions well beyond. It is a discussion in progress, defying early conclusions and final definition. It is an invitation to dialogue.

The studios presented also reflect the mix of local and international influences evident in the design field across disciplines in China. Their founders studied in China and overseas. Some are registered landscape architects in the United States and members of the American Society of Landscape Architects (ASLA). From clients to professionals, having travelled or studied abroad and being familiar with the global discourse and design practice is a shared commonality in China. The same applies to landscape architecture education, as Ron Henderson describes in detail in his essay *A Profession in the Making*. When, after decades of disruptions and instability, landscape architecture programmes reopened again at the turn of the millennium, the first generation of returnees from overseas studies in Europe and the United States played a vital role in the renaissance of the profession. Today Liu Binyi, Wang Xiangrong and Yu Kongjian together with Yang Rui and Zhu Yufan shape the discourse in Chinese landscape architecture nationally and internationally as heads of department at China's leading universities.

Chinese landscape architecture has many dimensions. On the one hand, it is a young profession trained in new academic programmes, intrinsically interwoven into global networks and challenged to find resilient solutions for high-density urban living in this millennium of urbanisation, most prominent in China. At the same time, China looks back on a centuries-old tradition of classical gardens. In comparison to Europe and later the New World, where garden art gradually evolved from classical private gardens and estates to early civic parks into the scope of modern landscape architecture, the historical continuity and gradual transformation of park design alongside societal change is missing in China, and past and present appear seemingly unrelated. As is often the case when in search of identity and synchronicity with history, neoclassical style gardens have become en vogue in recent years in residential landscape design. It has not been the first landscape design trend in China, and it will not be the last. But the question beyond the replication of appearances remains: Is there a defining essence in Chinese landscape aesthetics over the centuries that is still relevant today and can inform modern-day design?

The founders of the studios provide a spectrum of answers regarding the synthesis of tradition and modernity and the interrelation of landscape architecture and Chinese aesthetics and philosophy. In addition, the essay on *Chinese Landscape Aesthetics* by Claudia Westermann illustrates the Chinese perception of 'landscape' in literature and art. As the subtitle *The Exchange and Nurturing of Emotions* suggests, the Chinese view on 'landscape' differs significantly from that of the West – starting from the fact that the Chinese language has no word for 'landscape', since landscape is not perceived as a physical object independent from the observer, but as a spiritual experience. The literal translation of the Chinese characters for landscape architect is 'scenery view designer'. As the term implies, landscape design is not primarily regarded as the creation of an object or shape, but as an entity which naturally engages the viewers with their body and mind as participants.

Similarly, a fact most prominent across all featured studios is the notion of public space as a stage – a performative space for experience. Although the studios differ in approach and terminology, they all launch the idea of designing a public space as a framework which only comes to life when it is inhabited by users and open for their reinterpretation and interaction with space. The overall composition appears to take a back seat, leaving the stage to seasons, light and shadow, the reflections on still or the sound of moving water, and the tactile quality of materials. The designs are described through the lens of the viewer and their experience in space. From guiding visitors through sequences of landscape scenes, to recalling 'traditional lifestyles' in the mind of the observer, to evoking an inner sensory vocabulary or encouraging interactive play through smart technologies – the common denominator is the perception of users as engaged observers and participants in the designed landscape.

Disruption and continuity in parallel with progress and innovation characterise many aspects of China's society today. The speed of China's economic growth and urbanisation seems to defy gradual transitions. The cities have equally experienced decades of radical transformation. For millennia, China was an agrarian society; industrialisation in China happened over a century later than in the West. China's opening and reform policies began a mere forty years ago. The China of today, which is known for its megacities and more than a hundred cities of over one million inhabitants, is still a recent phenomenon. Most of China's current city dwellers grew up in the countryside or in low-rise urban quarters, later either moving to the city or staying and observing the city fabric changing as neighbourhoods and townships were turned into high-density urban areas. The late but rapid urbanisation bears consequences for both urban and rural life, and for landscape architecture as its agent.

As China's cities are transforming, so are the rites and rituals of public space use. Compared to the established set of recreational practices and user demands in the West, Chinese society is still in search of a suitable vocabulary of urban space. Most, if not all, of the projects presented in this book raise questions concerning the present status of landscape architecture design and hint towards future scenarios of public space: Which spaces do Chinese cities need today and how can the city fabric be transformed in an inclusive and resilient manner? What can public space design offer to the citizens today, and what will be their potential future needs? Hence, many of the projects are experimental in nature and are prototypes for change.

High-density urban living, the related demand for recreational space and the high frequency of use are additional drivers for growth and innovation. After decades of urban expansion, Chinese urban planning and design are re-evaluating inner-city planning, from adaptive reuse of former industrial sites to waterfront rejuvenation projects and micro-regeneration of historic city quarters. The new and complex task of fine-tuned inner-city renewal has changed the landscape architecture portfolio in China. Placemaking has come to the forefront of the discourse. Projects became smaller. New stakeholders have come into play and public participation is gaining momentum, as Jeff Hou argues in his essay on *Grounding a New Design Agency*. At the same time, China's countryside is suffering from the negative side-effects of China's growing urbanisation rates. Challenged by the rising inequality of living standards and economic prospects, the countryside needs new sustainable solutions, some of which are discussed in this book.

These are interesting times. The landscape architecture profession in China is the most vibrant and diverse it has ever been. The stakes are high, and the studios presented react with an encouraging spirit of optimism and innovation, radical at times and always rooted in the local context. Hopefully, this book will equally inspire, provoke debate and enhance cross-cultural dialogue.

Essay

A Profession in the Making

New Academic Programmes Redefining Landscape Architecture as a 21st Century Discipline

Ron Henderson

Landscape Architecture is a young profession in China, but an argument can be made that landscape architects have succeeded in making the discipline stronger in China than anywhere else in the world over the last two decades. A modern profession with an uncertain beginning in the mid-twentieth century grew upon the shoulders of China's agricultural legacy of working the earth, cultivating plants and harnessing waters as well as her rich tradition of gardens. These legacies have nurtured one of the most fertile cultures for landscape architecture in the world.

The inauguration of landscape architecture as a profession new to China, 1949–2000 – After the communist revolution, and for about half a century, most landscapes were implemented by bureaus which were municipal or provincial design teams under the auspices of the government. Teams of engineers, planners, architects, a few landscape architects and other professionals worked within the government structure to design and build cities, neighbourhoods, housing and facilities. The universities prepared students exclusively for work in these bureaus.

Degree programmes in the modern profession of landscape architecture began soon after the revolution. Although courses were held at Tsinghua University, Beijing in 1951, the first degrees were offered at Beijing Forestry University in 1952, at Nanjing Forestry University in 1956, and – under Urban Planning – at Tongji University, Shanghai in 1958. In contrast, the first programme in the United States, at Harvard, had been founded half a century earlier, in 1900.

From the 1960s to the late 1970s, Chinese urban development was stagnant. Almost nothing was built. With Deng Xiaoping's economic reform strategy in the late 1970s, China embarked on decades of rapid economic advances and urban development. The early years of Deng Xiaoping's reforms, from 1977 to 1980, also resulted in the extensive growth of universities, including the surge of landscape architecture programmes. Following this period of expansion, the number of programmes in China gradually increased to around 60 by the end of the 1980s with curricula primarily directed towards gardens rather than public landscapes and ecological planning.

In China, national ministries fund the academic programmes that are under their auspices. Landscape architecture programmes in Schools of Forestry are administered by the Bureau of Forests and Agriculture. Programmes in Schools of Architecture are administered by the Bureau of Construction. In a ministry reorganisation in 1996, many professional degree programmes were terminated by the Chinese government; among them almost all landscape architecture programmes. In the Chinese system of education, professions are ranked such that first-class professions are granted more academic resources, more programmes, and more leadership in commissioned projects and research. At this time, Landscape Architecture was a second-class sub-profession of Urban Planning, which meant that the academic and professional standing of the discipline was more limited compared to Category 1 professions such as Architecture.

When the mass cancellation happened, there had been about 60 landscape architecture programmes around the country. Of the faculties in Schools of Forestry or Agriculture, only Beijing Forestry University, Nanjing Forestry University, Shanghai Agriculture University and a few others were able to sustain their programmes. Almost all of the programmes in Architecture Schools ceased granting landscape architecture degrees, with only Tongji University able to continue, in part, by temporarily changing their programme to Tourism Management.

It was around this time, however, that three landscape architects who would become leaders of a 'new first generation' of landscape architects went to study abroad: Wang Xiangrong[1] to the University of Kassel in Germany, Yu Kongjian[2] to Harvard University and Hu Jie[3] to the University of Illinois in the United States. This group of landscape architects share a common academic heritage, as all are graduates of Beijing Forestry University which has, for over 70 years, been an anchor for the profession in China. In addition to this group, Liu Binyi[4] was a visiting scholar at Virginia Polytechnic University. These four landscape architects represent a cohort which would return to China with new ideas about landscape architecture, ecology, landscape planning and advanced computing to contribute to the growth and pedagogical development of landscape architecture at leading institutions: Beijing Forestry University, Peking University, Tsinghua University and Tongji University respectively. In addition, Zhu Yufan[5] earned the first Ph.D. in Landscape Architecture in China, from Beijing Forestry University in 1997.

The resurgence of landscape architecture as a twenty-first-century profession in China – The first decade of the new millennium, 2000–2010, saw a renewed growth in landscape architecture programmes. By 2011, there were around 70 programmes divided among schools of architecture, forestry and agriculture, including 25 graduate programmes and 45 undergraduate programmes. The sudden growth was caused by rapid urbanisation and environmental concerns demanding experts, of which there were simply too few in China. This led to a demand to educate more Chinese in the profession and to recruit talent and knowledge from abroad. In this period, many Chinese students of landscape architecture received their initial education in China and continued their postgraduate study in North America, Europe, and Australia. It was not only students and landscape professionals who went overseas, however. Municipal and provincial leaders and project developers also travelled the world to gain a deeper knowledge of best practices and successful projects to guide China's rapid development.

This growth of the profession also led to a remarkable volume of projects in the decade to 2010 – including high profile and internationally award-winning projects such as the Beijing Olympic Forest Park, Shanghai Expo, national ecological plan, national park and heritage protection initiatives, and new city districts around the nation – often directed by a small group of young landscape architects marshalling the talents of even younger project designers and staff.

Among this generation of new programmes in the first decade of the twenty-first century was the Master of Landscape Architecture at Tsinghua University, initiated in 2003. As the academic pipeline had been severed in the previous decade, China experienced a shortage of academic leaders to guide all new and re-established programmes. Tsinghua University looked abroad for leadership and appointed Laurie Olin, whose distinguished global practice and teaching at the University of Pennsylvania and Harvard University brought strong credentials to the programme. I joined Laurie Olin as part of the inaugural faculty where I became the first non-Chinese full-time faculty appointment in the College of Architecture.

An important legislative accomplishment in 2011 established Landscape Architecture as an even stronger profession. Through successful advocacy by landscape architecture leaders, led by Yang Rui[6] at Tsinghua University and Liu Binyi[4] at Tongji University, Landscape Architecture was elevated to a first-class discipline on par with Architecture and Planning. This designation brought increased academic and professional resources from the national government and a surge in new programmes. By 2013, there were around 180 landscape architecture programmes.

The turn of the twenty-first century witnessed an increasing demand for environmental and urban design leadership in the rapidly urbanising cities. Today, landscape architects in China have a stronger role in the design of cities and territories than in almost any other nation in the world, and it happened very quickly. This success is largely internal to China, however, and the emergence of Chinese landscape architects into global academic and design leadership remains nascent.

As we pass into the third decade of the millennium, new private landscape architecture practices which are the progeny of this most recent phase of urbanisation – such as those represented in this book – continue to advance and diversify the landscape architecture profession in China. There is a revived confidence explicit in the work of this group which is defining landscapes with their sensibility for public space, material explorations, a nuanced resolution of scale and plants in the urban context, and a strong commitment to designing liveable places for people. It is to be expected that this group, and others in their generation, building upon their rich global design experiences and expertise, will emerge as global landscape architecture design leaders in the world's first urban century.

[1] Wang Xiangrong, Dean and Professor at the School of Landscape Architecture at Beijing Forestry University, Beijing
[2] Yu Kongjian, Dean and Professor at the Graduate School of Landscape Architecture at Peking University, Beijing
[3] Hu Jie, Vice-President, Beijing Tsinghua Tongheng Urban Planning and Design Institute, Beijing
[4] Liu Binyi, Professor and Chair of the Department of Landscape Architecture at CAUP at Tongji University, Shanghai
[5] Zhu Yufan, Professor and Deputy Head of the Department of Landscape Architecture at Tsinghua University, Beijing
[6] Yang Rui, Chair of the Department of Landscape Architecture at the School of Architecture at Tsinghua University, Beijing

Essay

Chinese Landscape Aesthetics

The Exchange and Nurturing of Emotions

Claudia Westermann

And high over the willows, the fine birds sing to each other, and listen,
Crying – 'Kwan, Kuan', for the early wind, and the feel of it.
The wind bundles itself into a bluish cloud and wanders off.
Over a thousand gates, over a thousand doors are the sounds of spring singing,
And the Emperor is at Ko.
Excerpt of The River Song, by Li Bai, 8th century CE, translated by Ezra Pound[1]

The Chinese language has a variety of terms that are typically translated into English as *landscape*. There is 景观 jǐng guān – scenery view. An old meaning of 景 jǐng is light, luminous. So, literally 景观 jǐng guān means luminous view. The term is generally used when referring to foreign educational programmes in landscape architecture. Traditionally, university departments in China indicate an engagement with ideas of landscape with the characters 园林 yuán lín – garden forests. These are the characters for the classical Chinese gardens. The characters 风景 fēng jǐng, that literally translate to wind scenery, or wind light as the French sinologist François Jullien suggests[2], are also fairly common. Landscape in painting is referred to as 山水 shān shuǐ – mountain(s) water(s) – but also as 山川 shān chuān – mountain(s) river(s). The attentive reader will have noticed that the Chinese language always employs a pair of characters to refer to landscape. Likewise, there is always an in-between that indicates space for agency.

You see a white path disappearing into the blue and think of travelling on it.
You see the glow of setting sun over level waters and dream of gazing on it.
You see hermits and mountain dwellers and think of lodging with them.
You see cliffs by lucid water or streams over rocks, and long to wander there.
Excerpt of The Lofty Message of Forest and Streams by Guo Xi, ca. 1080 CE[3]

Landscapes allow viewers to travel, to dream of gazing, dwell and wander, suggested the celebrated painter Guo Xi in the treatise entitled *The Lofty Message of Forest and Streams*, written around 1080 CE. *The Chinese wind light and mountain(s) water(s)* that refer to landscape as mentioned above reflect the fact that the Chinese concept of landscape developed in conversation with poetry and painting. Indeed, the etymological development of the terms cannot be separated from the interaction with an art that goes beyond the perceptual. Wind touches us. Art in China is affectual. Calligraphy, which is closely related to painting, is the prime example, highlighting that art in China involves body and mind. As painting, calligraphy forms through skilfully performed movements that are learnt over decades of practice. Likewise, art is not appreciated from a distance but again engaged with. It is touched, written and stamped on.

In Europe, the meaning of *landscape* has also evolved in connection with painting. The defining development, however, took place only in the sixteenth century when the Renaissance initiated the interest in the depiction of undisturbed nature. Before this, landscape painting did not exist as a discipline in Europe. Reflecting this relatively late development, a contemporary definition of landscape is: "the appearance of the area of land, which the eye can view at once; the aspect of a country, or a picture or photograph representing it; the production of such pictures or photographs."[4] While the term *landscape* can be found in European literature of earlier centuries, its concept at the time also related to questions of representation. *Landscape* is formed by the noun *land* and the ancient Indo-Germanic verb *scapjan*, which in its meaning is close to *shaping*.[5] However, *shape*, as unity in form, indicating something that differentiates itself from other things, emphasises borders. The idea of a cut-out that is present in the contemporary meaning of *landscape* reflects the fixation of the term *landscape* during the Renaissance, when concepts of part-whole relations were discussed that are inherent in a mechanical interpretation of nature and the living. In consonance with the Renaissance ideas that also form the basis of linear perspective, the concept of *landscape* similarly further developed with an emphasis on the visual sense. *Landscape* depicts an ideal. Its ideas, developed in painting, were later transmitted to physical spaces and influenced what the typical Western perception of landscape is.

Considering the different contexts that facilitated the creation of the concepts of landscape in China and Europe, it is not surprising that the Chinese terms for landscape do not reflect what Europeans typically associate with the idea of landscape. For example, it was only in the eighteenth century that China learned of linear perspective. It is most lucidly termed 透视 tòu shì – through view. Chinese landscape paintings until then used oblique projection with shifting viewpoints, referred to by the terms 远近 yuǎn jìn – near far. These paintings engage the viewer in an oscillation between the poles of the far and the near, and the fixed and the flowing. There is no separation between these poles. There is connection. China did not frame paintings. Landscape painting scrolls were explicitly conceived for interaction with the viewer. The Chinese near-far 'perspective' appears to take this interaction into account. The view lines point outwards, and viewpoints – shifting at short intervals – draw the viewer in again and again into a different scene. The viewer enters into relations with a new set of scenes as she or he moves along. There is no fixation as the figures and objects seem to shift constantly, entering into new relations as the viewer unrolls the painting. In fact, Chinese landscape scrolls resist the viewer. They engage people with both bodies and minds as participants. Chinese landscapes in the physical world act in a similar manner.

Chinese art did not emphasise artists with divine vision as mediators between the viewers and the world. Instead, it stressed the function of the artwork as an interface, making viewers participants in the world. The German-Korean philosopher Byung-Chul Han goes as far as suggesting that artists in China have perfected the art of 'absenting' themselves from their works to grant agency to those who appreciate the works.[5] According to Han, it is this kind of absence which allows the work of art to perform, to act, and to engage the viewers, connecting them to the larger world. Painters also left blank space on their scrolls for others to imprint their stamps. Signs of appreciation, these stamped images become part of the painting and communicate with it. It is within the context of the work of art as interface to an experiencing of the world that Guo Xi's text, quoted further above, is to be understood.

That works of art should be created to act as mediators between viewers and the world, or rather between living and acting inhabitants and the world, was maintained over many hundreds of years. In the famous Chinese painting manual *Mustard Seed Garden: Manual of Painting*, which was written between 1679 and 1701, around 600 years after Guo Xi's text, the painting apprentices are told that "Figures should, in fact, be depicted in such a way that people looking at a painting wish they could change places with them."[6] These ideas, which have been fostered in an engagement with the painting and simultaneously the making of landscapes in the classical Chinese gardens, still linger on in the Chinese landscapes of today.

We are touched by landscape. A scene gives birth to emotions (景生情 jǐng shēng qíng). Landscape induces a process of emotional exchange between the 'scene' itself and someone who takes part in the scene, may he or she wander, dwell, or dream of gazing. Wind and light, and waters and mountains make the scenery. It is not inactive. It is flowing with the waters, halting with the mountains. In the images of light and wind the ephemeral is inscribed. Time is part of space. The scene performs. Both human beings wandering in the scene and the scene itself are active agents in a process that the Chinese scholar Yù Yuán 郁沅 refers to as emotion-scene blending (情景交融 qíng jǐng jiāo róng).[7]

Chinese landscapes nurture emotions and emerge through affection. They live within the sensorial experience of those who come to engage with them in an infinite play between the mountains and waters, light and wind.

[1] Ezra Pound and Timothy Billings (ed.). *Cathay: A Critical Edition*. New York: Fordham University Press, 2019, p. 37.
[2] François Jullien. *Living Off Landscape: Or, the Unthought-of in Reason*. Lanham, Maryland: Rowman & Littlefield International, [2014] 2018, p. 46.
[3] Susan Bush and Hsio-Yen Shih. *Early Chinese Texts on Painting*. Hong Kong: Hong Kong University Press, 2012, p. 153.
[4] Allied Chambers. 'Landscape', In *The Chambers Dictionary*. Edinburgh: Chambers Harrap Publishers Ltd., 1998.
[5] Byung-Chul Han, *Abwesen: zur Kultur und Philosophie des Fernen Ostens*. Berlin: Merve, 2007.
[6] Mai-Mai Sze and Kai Wang. *The Mustard Seed Garden: Manual of Painting*, Princeton, NJ: Princeton University Press, [1679-1701] 1978, p. 220.
[7] Yù Yuán 郁沅, On the three types of emotion-scene blending 情景交融三类型论, *Journal of Southeast University (Philosophy and Social Science)* 东南大学学报 (哲学社会科学版), (3):89, 2007, pp. 89–94.

Grounding a New Design Agency

Rural/Urban Experimentations in China

Jeffrey Hou

In recent decades, the narrative of built environment planning and design in China has been one of rapid expansion and exponential growth. In a short period, remarkable projects have been built at scales and speed that are inconceivable elsewhere in the world, with perhaps the exception of parts of the Middle East. These larger-than-life projects serve as symbols of power and prestige. They present once-in-a-lifetime opportunities for architects and landscape architects seeking commissions. As the speed of Chinese urbanisation began to decelerate, however, and as urban sites became increasingly saturated, a different kind of experiment has emerged in both the cities and the countryside. Specifically, in contrast to the iconic design trophies, a new crop of humanitarian, bottom-up and civic-oriented practices is redefining the role of design in Chinese society.

Starting with the cities, as large-scale demolitions have scraped away large sections of urban fabrics from Beijing to Shanghai, some remaining enclaves of old living quarters are now experiencing a different kind of upgrade. In Shanghai, for instance, a policy for so-called **micro-regeneration** was launched at the subdistrict level in 2016, to preserve many heritage communities and improve living conditions while the increasing cost of relocation and the lengthy process of resettlement was also at play.[1] The approach of micro-scale improvements proved to be a viable alternative with the added benefits of environmental sustainability. These projects also became the testing ground for community engagement and participation in the planning and design process and collaboration among a host of actors and institutions.

The renovation of Guizhouli led by Tong Ming, an Architecture Professor at Tongji University, was one such project that I visited in 2018 along with a group of curious practitioners who had just listened to a presentation by Prof. Tong. On our short and impromptu visit to the neighbourhood, we talked with residents as we walked around the neighbourhood alleyways and courtyards. The design interventions unfolded in front of us as we watched the locals following their daily routines. Developed in consultation with residents, the design interventions allowed and even supported everyday uses of neighbourhood spaces, including drying clothing and blankets out in the open as well as the operation of small businesses at the gateways. Rather than cosmetic changes, the acupunctural interventions focused on improving functionalities and supporting existing uses through better organisation and by creating more welcoming thresholds.

Urban gardening initiatives were part of the strategies for micro-regeneration in Shanghai. In An Shan Si Chun, one of the largest working-class neighbourhoods in the city, the lack of public space was one of the problems facing the community. The subdistrict government invited Liu Yuelai and the Clover Nature School to lead a project that would meet the needs of residents for leisure and family activities and environmental education. The project resulted in the creation of a community garden in the neighbourhood.[2]

Rather than just a green open space, the garden was envisioned as a model for community building. Featured in this volume, the Clover Nature School is a unique model that integrates design, education and community engagement through urban gardening. Since 2014, the organisation has been working with a multitude of stakeholders in the city to promote urban gardening, including local districts, communities and commercial developers.

The Knowledge & Innovation Community Garden (KICG), a showcase of the Clover Nature School, served as a prime example of how urban gardens can provide multiple social, environmental and educational benefits. The project involves collaboration among multiple partners pooling together financial support and planning and design expertise with the participation of volunteers. In addition to the garden plots, an indoor classroom structure provides educational programming for schoolchildren as well as opportunities for social events. The grounds of KICG further include rain gardens, habitats for pollinators and places for community gatherings and leisure activities, forming a green refuge in a dense urban setting. On my many visits to the site, the gardens at KICG never looked the same each time I visited, much like a living being regenerating and evolving organically over time, similar to many other community gardens elsewhere.

Besides urban sites, **rural experimentations** have also been a vehicle for growing design innovations in China. For years, an increasing number of notable design projects have emerged in remote rural villages to address unique opportunities for local adaptations and designs that address 'limited resources of budget, craft and technology.'[3] The work of Rural Urban Framework (RUF) has been exemplary in this regard. In the Jintai Village Reconstruction Project, located in Sichuan Province, RUF took the opportunity of a site obliterated by heavy rainfall and landslides and set out to incorporate many landscape features including a permeable paving system, rainwater collection system, reed bed wastewater treatment, constructed wetland and underground biogas energy system, in addition to architectural design for passive environmental control. The design also created space for animal rearing and rooftop farming.[4]

As important and innovative these design interventions are, however, the multitude and magnitude of issues faced by rural regions in China require much more than just design interventions. Specifically, the challenges of rural-urban disparity, economic and population decline, pollution and the loss of arable land can hardly be addressed by landscape design alone. It is in this context that the work of Fu Yingbin Studio stands out as distinct and highly significant. Unlike many projects in the rural context that are still preoccupied with formal and spatial expressions, the studio's projects have focused on holistic solutions to address systemic issues facing the rural communities and environments including economic and financial challenges. The studio's work is a far cry from the vast number of architectural follies that do not perform much other than exploiting the picturesque rural context.

As with all pioneering work, there were inevitably missteps and lessons learned through these undertakings. In Shanghai, many of the earliest attempts in neighbourhood improvements have been short-lived if not derailed or failed. For instance, in one project that tried to reorganise a crowded neighbourhood street to create more amenities for the neighbours, the new plants were soon stolen after the completion of the construction, and the widened pavements were again occupied by motorbikes and household items. In another project, residents of a renovated apartment building complained angrily about the intrusion of visitors who flocked to see the design that went viral on social media. The projects in the countryside had their share of issues and struggles as well, including negotiating with conflicting stakeholders and learning to work patiently with local constituents, materials and institutions.

In many ways, these struggles and challenges are just as important as the material outcomes that are depicted in this volume. One may argue that it is precisely through these challenges and struggles that learning and understanding took place for the different actors and stakeholders. For landscape architects and other design professionals in particular, this included the nuances of working with communities and institutions outside their professional comfort zones. It is also through these projects and processes that the boundaries of practices are pushed and the complexity of social and environmental realities is confronted. It is based on these encounters that assumptions of design and professional practice are challenged and sometimes debunked.

The work of Fu Yingbin Studio, Clover Nature School and many others in this volume represents a process through which a new design agency is being grounded in China, an approach that puts design in service of community building, local economic development and reinvestment in place, people and processes. More than form-making and material expressions, the projects showcased in this volume serve as windows into ways in which landscape architecture practices now intersect with the full social, economic and environmental complexity of contemporary China. While the projects themselves may seem modest in size and scale compared with their more high-profile counterparts, their meanings and presence are no less significant.

[1] Xiaohua Zhong and Ho Hon Leung, "Exploring Participatory Microregeneration as Sustainable Renewal of Built Heritage Community: Two Case Studies in Shanghai," Sustainability 11, 1617 (2019): 1–15.

[2] Zhong and Leung, "Exploring Participatory Microregeneration."

[3] Joshua Bolchover and John Lin, Rural Urban Framework: Transforming the Chinese Countryside (Basel, Switzerland: Birkhäuser, 2014): 116.

[4] Rural Urban Framework, "Jintai Village Reconstruction," in Critical Care: Architecture and Urbanism for a Broken Planet, eds. Angelika Fitz, Elke Krasny and Architekturzentrum Wien (Cambridge, MA, and London, England: Architekturzentrum Wien and the MIT Press, 2019): 140–145.

Eight Perspectives

Z+T Studio

Participatory Landscapes

Shanghai

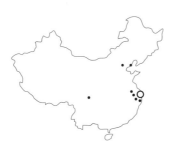

Z+T Studio

Shanghai

Founder: Zhang Dong, Tang Ziying
Founded: 2009
Team: 20–45
Location: Shanghai
Portfolio: environmental design, public parks and plazas, playground design, resort design, residential design
In-house: Biophilic Lab, Art Workshop

Z+T Studio was founded in 2009 by Zhang Dong and Tang Ziying. Zhang and Tang's extensive professional experience both in the United States and China laid the foundation for the Shanghai studio, which integrates the perspectives and sensitivities of East and West. Countering the quantity-dominated trend in China's design field, Z+T Studio was the first landscape practice in China to foster a deliberately moderate-sized studio team and office culture. Widely acknowledged in the landscape industry for their thorough and inventive transdisciplinary approach to design, Z+T Studio is one of the leading landscape architecture practices in China today.

The team of members from diverse professional backgrounds, including landscape architects, architects, urban planners, artists, horticulturists and ecologists, is engaged in projects ranging from masterplanning, ecological restoration and environmental research, to public urban parks and commercial plazas, and tourism and hospitality design.

Two subsidiaries established by Z+T Studio in recent years – the Art Workshop, a full-scale mock-up and manufacturing workshop for outdoor furniture and structures designed by Z+T Studio, and the Biophilic Lab, an in-house environmental research and study group – are instrumental to the design process and construction quality of Z+T Studio's work. Together, they serve as both technical support for the projects and as a cradle of new ideas and innovative solutions.

In conversation with Tang Ziying and Zhang Dong about public space design in a society in transformation, participatory design and in-house manufacturing.

Z+T Studio is one of the leading landscape architecture practices in China. Your studio model inspired an entire generation of young designers. Looking back today at your own beginnings in landscape architecture, what influenced you? How would you define your roots in the profession?

Tang Ziying We have very different roots but also hold many shared experiences. Our different perspectives always make for a good debate, without ever losing our common ground.

Zhang Dong is the Co-founder and Principal of Z+T Studio. He is interested in both the creative impulse at the genesis of each project and the thorough fine-tuning and technical feasibility of the initial ideas. Having grown up in a small town in Central China and studied and worked both in China and the United States, Dong has witnessed the dramatic social, cultural and economic changes in China over the past decades. This experience forms the basis of Zhang Dong's explorations of landscape design as a means to improve people's everyday quality of life in a fast-changing society like China. He holds a Master of Landscape Architecture from Chongqing University School of Architecture and a Master of Landscape Architecture from the University of Massachusetts, Amherst, USA.

Tang Ziying is the Co-founder and Principal of Z+T Studio. She is interested in the implications of different social and spatial conditions on landscape design. In her creative work, she addresses project design not merely from a visual perspective, but from people's bodily and sensory experiences and the symbolic and cultural connotations of the place. She believes that each design intervention should be based on site-specific spatial organisation and innovation in materiality. Tang Ziyang is an honourable member of the American Society of Landscape Architects (ASLA). She holds a Master of Urban Planning and Environmental Design from Peking University, Beijing, and a Master of Landscape Architecture from the University of Massachusetts, Amherst, USA.

‹‹ Jia Zhu Li Courtyard, Ningbo

Zhang Dong (l.), Tang Ziying (r.) – Z+T Studio ››

Zhang Dong I grew up in a small town in the mountains of Central China. We had no park in our city. To be honest, when the acceptance letter from Chongqing University arrived, which assigned me to the landscape architecture programme, no one in my family knew what landscape architecture was, myself included. And so, it all began.

The experience of Chongqing was truly mindblowing for me. At that time already, Chongqing was a big city bursting with life, and I started to gain a first impression of the fabric and meaning of urban landscapes and parks. Ziying and I met during our studies and later moved to the United States together for a second master's degree. And once again, the urban landscape was completely different. At that time, parks in China were still designed as classical-style gardens, with walkways and pagodas. In fact, they were not even real parks, but rather classic gardens open to the public. In the US, we learned about community parks and what they can mean to the city.

Tang Ziying We realised the relevance of a park as an urban space, but also how park design differs according to the make-up of society, both in comparison between the US and China but also within China over the course of time. If you look at parks in China right now, they are very different from parks ten or even twenty years ago. Because society is changing, the economy is changing and even the family structure is changing. That might as well be the reason why we designed so many playgrounds at Z+T Studio. When raising children in a high-density city, the demand for playscapes in parks is huge.

Zhang Dong People's expectations of park design and use have changed significantly. Twenty years ago, people visited parks for a stroll, to observe a beautiful scenery or to take pictures. It was like 'scenery-picking'. People weren't allowed to bring food or drinks to a park. But today, people go to a park for a picnic. You can walk as you please, play football, fly kites.

Tang Ziying How people use a park today is very different compared to forty years ago, when China opened up. We are still in the midst of this transformation process. It is still changing.

I grew up in a mid-sized city, ten times larger than Dong's. We had a park. The parks of this era were called People's Parks. Our city park had two parts: a botanical garden and a zoo, and sure, a lake for boating. My father

We realised the relevance of a park as an urban space but also how park design differs according to the make-up of society, both in comparison between the US and China but also within China over the course of time.

How people use a park today is very different compared to forty years ago, when China opened up. We are still in the midst of this transformation process. It is still changing.

was a painter. We often went to the park. He would sketch tigers while we enjoyed the flowers and trees. There were even bonsai. But we also had mountains running right into the city and often went hiking. There were no paths. We were literally hiking in nature. We also occasionally visited classical Chinese gardens. I remember at school, after field trips to these parks, we had to write an essay about our appreciation. It is all quite intellectual. You either know the poem that a garden scene refers to or you are lost. It all depends on your knowledge of history and literature. Frankly speaking, I never quite enjoyed those types of parks.

I do think landscape architecture is very different from other art disciplines. It is not only visual. There is no need to fully intellectually understand a landscape. Look at our kids. We usually bring them to our parks. They run around, they enjoy the place, sure they appreciate the water, the flowers, or something beautiful. But if you would ask them: What do you see? What do you like? They certainly would not be able to describe it. But that doesn't matter. All that's important is that they enjoy the experience. An experience is not a visual phenomenon; an experience always arises through the senses and the body.

How would you value these early experiences of landscapes and their influence on your design today?

Zhang Dong Our own experience has definitely influenced how we think and act in our practice. When I was young, around the age of my boy now, my family was not yet living in this small town. We lived in a farmhouse far from the village. I had to walk to school every day, crossing a small mountain. There was only a trail, no real path, and a creek. Often on my way home, I would walk right through the creek and catch a fish. That was so much fun. When it rained, the trail became completely muddy, and many rivulets of rainwater would trickle down the hills. I still remember the playful flow of all these small waterlines. They looked very similar to the Meandering Creek we designed in Cloud Paradise Park. Sure, these kinds of early experiences continue to influence our design today.

Tang Ziying Dong had a very different experience in his early years than I did. He grew up so freely in the rural countryside. I wish our children could have similar opportunities to discover the world and explore their skills. This freedom to play is also what we strive for in our designs.

An experience is not a visual phenomenon; an experience always arises through the senses and the body.

Zhang Dong I will share one more memory, which later turned into a 'designed' experience. Every winter during school holidays, we needed to go into the mountains to collect firewood for cooking for the whole year. Later, we would pile all the branches in front of our home, layer after layer, into huge piles. When we had finished, we were allowed to jump on these soft humps. Decades later, when we were designing the Jumping Clouds in Paradise Park, it brought back the memory of this childhood experience. Sure, it is not the same. It can and it should never be exactly the same. But the core is. It is a real experience – a real bodily experience.

In 2018, Z+T Studio published a compendium titled Participatory Landscapes. How is this approach reflected in your project design?

Tang Ziying Perhaps this first requires clarification, that the term is not 'lost in translation'. We don't use the term 'participatory' in the same way it is employed in the States, implying people's direct engagement during the design process.

Zhang Dong It's a different mindset here in China. We are considered the 'experts' and expected to design the park. The way we see participation is that we invite people to participate through the way they use the park.

Tang Ziying When we design a park, we only design a base, a frame, a context and then we need 'actors'. Only when people use the places do they become active. We prepare the space, but they turn it into reality.

Zhang Dong It is like creating a stage. When designing a park, we for sure have the users in mind and anticipate how the spaces will be used. But when real people come, half of them might use it in the way it was intended and others in a way one would never have expected. It's exactly this participation that makes parks an active part of society.

Tang Ziying We don't want to control too much. We rather want to share an observation. In the design for U-Centre Plaza for example, we found out that there had been a train crossing in the past and people needed to wait for ten minutes at the junction. In the plaza design, we bring back this 'ten minutes of pausing' through a rotating platform at the centre of the square. As people wait for ten minutes, the scenery around them

Only when people use the places do they become active. We prepare the space, but they turn it into reality. It's exactly this participation that makes parks an active part of society.

We plant a seed, a potential moment to engage – but how to fill it in, use it, or ignore it, is completely up to the people.

Team gathering at the Art Workshop of Z+T Studio – the in-house manufacturing workshop in a factory hall adjacent to the studio ∧

changes. We observed young couples, for example, play with this change by staying at opposite sides and letting the platform move them apart. We plant a seed, a potential moment to engage – but how to fill it in, use it, or ignore it, is completely up to the people.

Participatory design as a trigger for freedom in park use?

Tang Ziying Yes, but also allowing this freedom to happen in the first place. Our project sites aren't free from restrictions and limitations – far from it. U-Centre is a commercial plaza with all the related restraints on green cover and commercial requirements concerning view lines and people flow. Interfering by manipulating the ground was our 'trick' to create an opportunity for participation within the given constraints. It is the same at the Meandering Creek that Dong mentioned before. In technical terms, it is an emergency vehicle route, which crosses the play-scape. Fortunately, it was on a subtle slope. The artificial creek is made of concrete and the small rivulets are shallow. No conflict of interest – it is a win-win for both parties.

Zhang Dong There is a saying in China: 'seeking the sweetness in the bitterness'. You need to create fun. You need to pursue happiness while suffering. I think many of our designs have this attitude of finding the 'sweetness' and positivity in every project. The site might be challenging and the possibilities limited, but we put our creativity into making it joyful and pleasant, like turning the shortcomings of a less mature landscape construction sector into a chance to establish our own Art Workshop.

What role does Z+T's in-house Art Workshop play in your projects?

Tang Ziying We had this dream of having our own manufacturing work-shop right from the founding of our studio. When studying at UMass, I was enrolled in a sculpture studio where I observed artists who hired a crew to help test design again and again, study the materials and produce mock-ups. That's the perfect way for me to work. Back in China, we repeatedly encountered difficulties when realising our designs, especially when it came to structures and element design. Ordinary constructors in China won't do that type of work properly; and sculptors can't do it because they don't have the mechanical equipment at hand.

There is a saying in China: 'seeking the sweetness in the bitterness'. I think many of our designs have this attitude of finding the 'sweetness' and positivity in every project.

Zhang Dong The workshop also helps when communicating with clients. Usually, there are three questions one needs to be able to answer: 'Can you build it? How much will it cost? And how difficult will it be to maintain it?' If you can't answer these three basic questions, no one will endorse and build your design – and with the Art Workshop we can.

Tang Ziying It is very rewarding and different from only drawing and having your ideas built by someone else. The Art Workshop is located in a factory hall next door to our studio, and our team can study materials, test technical details and do mock-ups there first-hand.

You recently returned to China from a sabbatical year in the US. Which new reflections and observations are you carrying with you this time?

Zhang Dong There are many differences, to be sure. Something which struck us the most when revisiting the community parks, which we talked about before, was the difference in park life. In the US, most people seem to visit a park on weekends or special occasions as a music festival or the like. In a big city such as New York, that might be different. But in China, people go to a park every day and often even repeatedly. In the morning they go for exercise, during the day for play, in the evening for a stroll. They say 'The Future is Asian' and I also believe that we are about to develop a model for high-density urban living in China and across Asia. Sure, all regions are different. But beyond differences there is the commonality of growing urbanity. I see Asia as a big laboratory for future urban living. There was a king in China around 2000 years ago. He said: 'We are an ancient civilisation, but our mission is to seek something new.' I believe Chinese society is very entrepreneurial in its core and always ready to progress and look for something new, and potentially better.

Tang Ziying I believe landscape architecture is very closely related to society and culture. It is impossible to separate these aspects from one another. In my opinion, this interrelation defines the core of landscape architecture and distinguishes the profession from any other. It is not just about a physical condition one may study; there is something deeper one needs to understand. If one doesn't reach this level, the design remains superficial. It may solve an issue, but it will never fit the culture really deeply and be meaningful to the community.

I see Asia as a big laboratory for future urban living. They say 'The Future is Asian' and I also believe that we are about to develop a model for high-density urban living in China and across Asia.

Landscape architecture is very closely related to society and culture. In my opinion, this interrelation defines the core of landscape architecture and distinguishes the profession from any other.

Modifications of Flow
Art Workshop

Type: residential and commercial courtyard, public plaza

Size: varies

Year: 2016

Approach Water has always been at the core of classical Chinese garden art and landscape paintings and so it is in the work of Z+T Studio, yet in a modern interpretation. The selection of water elements portrayed typifies Z+T Studio's craft of 'making water speak'. Prototyped, tested and manufactured in-house at the Art Workshop of Z+T Studio, the meticulously shaped stone reliefs set the stage for the natural element to reveal its inherent qualities from reflection to distortion, and from tranquillity to vividness.

Royal Territory At Royal Territory in Hangzhou, a linear water sculpture forms the centre of the courtyard. It depicts an abstracted topography of Qiantang River and its surrounding mountains. The subtle slope engraved into the relief of the sculpture ensures the slow motion of the water through the courtyard, creating a poetic miniature scene of a river flowing through gorges,

while the reflections on the still water surface visually enlarge the confined space of the yard.

Yue-Yuan Courtyard The water feature at Yue-Yuan Courtyard in Suzhou is designed as a representation of the lasting force of water. The artificial creek line made of monolithic granite rock artfully simulates the natural hydrological processes. Meandering through the courtyard, its flow resembles the movement of water across the Earth's surface for millions of years, transforming the land into rivers and valleys.

The Park The spray and sound of waves at the beach are the theme of the animated water tables at The Park in Suzhou. A pair of custom-designed engines embedded into the platforms create gentle waves which dynamically spill over the edge of the water tables, inviting park users to touch and play with the water or simply observe its sparkles in the sunshine.

Royal Territory – negative mountain relief ⌃

Yue Yuan Courtyard – depicting a meandering creek ⌃

The Park – simulating waves at the beach ››

Cloud Paradise Park

Chengdu, Sichuan Province

Client: Wide Horizon Real Estate Development
Type: public park, playground

Size: 25,000 m²
Year: 2017

Place Cloud Paradise Park is the core recreational space at Luhu Lake in Luxelakes Water City in Chengdu. The water town, combining living, working, leisure and entertainment, spans across close to two square kilometres and has gained nationwide recognition as one of the leading eco-developments in China. Streams and lakes characterise the lush landscapes of the new town, recalling the traditional landscapes of the Chengdu Plain, fed by the ancient Dujiangyan irrigation system. In past decades, the water quality of the Chengdu's rivers and canals, many of them remnants of the centuries-old irrigation system, had deteriorated significantly and the water quality of natural stream feeding Luxelakes' water system was poor. Through a combination of scientific cultivation of aquatic plants and freshwater fish, Luxelakes succeeded in re-establishing a balanced aquatic ecosystem enabling the self-purification of the central lake. By 2014, the lake's water had reached nearly drinking water quality. Today, residents can swim in the lake or partake in water sports.

Approach The story of water also forms the main theme of Cloud Paradise Park. The various aggregation states of water are transformed into playscapes and features, encouraging play and simultaneous learning. The water system of the park is integrated into the overall ecological purifications methods of Luxelakes, with the central lake serving as the water source of all waterscapes.

Design The park tells the tale of the life of a drop of water through the seasons. The white inflatable trampoline marks the beginning of the water story as a metaphor for the clouds. The interactive fountain forms the second node. It represents rainfall. Four custom-made stationary

bicycles are designed to trigger water jets. From there the water flows along the meandering creek, which widens into the braided river that releases the water into the paddling pool. Water jets at the bottom of the pool, controlled by pad sensors at the side of the pool, encourage interactive play. At the central play area, a white semi-circular concrete slide, embedded into the existing topography, tells the story of snow. The dewdrop pavilion next to the slide continues the theme of winter, followed by the glacier corridor built by two mirror walls. A series of motion detectors installed along the passageway activate dripping water sounds when people pass by. As the last stop in the narrative, the bridge towards the promenade illustrates the pure reflective nature of ice. The water cycle of the playscape is directly connected to the central lake. Water is pumped from the lake and purified before starting its journey at the interactive fountain. After the paddling pool, the water is diverted into a wetland garden and filtered back into the lake.

Participatory design is at the core of Z+T Studio's design philosophy. Prior to the park's opening, the park management invited a dozen families to test the play facilities. Based on their feedback, the management together with Z+T Studio fine-tuned details and optimised maintenance strategies.

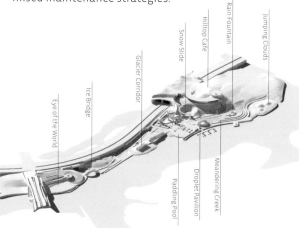

Eye of the World
Ice Bridge
Glacier Corridor
Snow Slide
Hilltop Cafe
Rain Fountain
Jumping Clouds
Paddling Pool
Droplet Pavilion
Meandering Creek

Meandering Creek ››

Topographic model ˄

Glacier Corridor ››

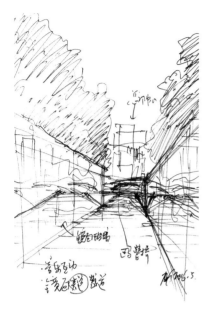

Ice Bridge ››

Water Droplet Pavilion ⌃

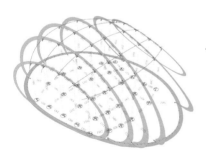

Art Workshop – mock-ups ›

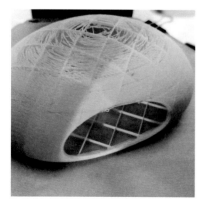

^ Meandering Creek and Braided River

‹ Clay model – flow studies

<< Jumping Clouds Trampoline   Semi-circular Snow Slide

Z+T Studio Cloud Paradise Park, Chengdu

63

Aranya Children's Farm

Beidaihe, Hebei Province

Client: Aranya Real Estate Co. Ltd.
Type: public park, playground

Size: 74,000 m²
Year: 2018

Place The project is part of Aranya Gold Coast Community Resort in Beidaihe district of Qinhuangdao. The resort town on the coast of China's Bohai Sea serves as a favourite seaside destination for the Jing-Jin-Ji Metropolitan Region, comprising Beijing, Tianjin and Hebei province. Aranya stands out for its community-focused approach to holiday town design. The mixed resort and residential development encompasses villas, condominiums and hotels and covers a total area of 220 hectares. Various new architectures line the wide sandy beaches of Beidaihe as landmarks of the community spirit and the holistic mission of Aranya, most notably the Seashore Chapel and Library by Vector Architects, the UCCA Dune Art Museum by Open Architecture and the Aranya Art Center by Neri & Hu. As with the communal buildings, Z+T Studio's children's farm and playground, located at the inland dunes, equally reflect the shared values of the community and serve the entire resort.

Approach The context and narrative of place form the foundation of Z+T Studio's design. At Aranya, an inland dune covered by a robinia forest has been the site earmarked for transformation. Over the last decade, the robinia forests along the coastal dunes of Qinhuangdao decreased by more than half and the remaining intact forest on-site became an isolated natural islet within the urban fabric. Today a protected coastal landscape, Robinia pseudoacacia aren't native to China either. Originating in North America, they were first introduced to China at the port city of Qingdao during the period of German concession, between 1898 and 1914, and quickly became the main afforestation tree species along the coastline of China's Yellow Sea. As Z+T reflects upon nature and change: "What is really natural? What is the core of this land? In the long river of history, everything changes constantly. When inland civilisation met marine civilisation, the dunes and deserted beaches were gradually inhabited. Dunes became dense forests; deserted beaches became farmsteads. Thousands of years of harmonious coexistence between Chinese culture and nature are full of legends of a better life. The legendary fable of Shan Hai Jing inspired people to become the spiritual source of continuous improvement of Chinese civilisation. In the famous chapter of the Tribute of Yu, the mystical figure Yu moved the mountains and reclaimed the sea, becoming a symbol of the virtues of perseverance and willpower in Chinese mythology. Changes in ecological awareness are still sparse today, but are on the rise. In our opinion, the soul of the site is neither the black locust forest nor the sand dunes or the coastal waters, but the changes in nature and world affairs, and the small but tenacious vitality of human beings."

Design The design proposal divides the site into two parts: a quiet meditation space in the robinia forest and an active children's farm and playground at the edge of the dune. Simplicity and minimalism in intervention and material choice define Z+T Studio's design for the meditation forest. Raised timber boardwalks and platforms float above the ground and shrub layer. Acrylic screens capture light and shadows, inviting passers-by to feel the changes of light and wind in nature while walking in the forest. By contrast, the activity park draws on inspiration from the Classics of Mountains and Seas (Shan Hai Jing), a geographical and cultural account of pre-Qin China, including a bestiary known to all Chinese. When the mythological creatures of Shan Hai Jing met modern leisure design, fishbone pavilions, eel benches, starfish flower fields, conch climbing structures, and octopus slides swarmed. Rainwater is collected at a wetland pond. Open channels and interactive play devices encourage children to lift up the water and irrigate the vegetable fields. The narrow triangle between the forested dune and the road became a children's farm uniting fairytale and play.

Fishbone Pavilion – forest playground ››

‹ Meditation Forest – simplicity of materials – wire mesh and acrylic screen

‹ Forest Playground – hill slides and driftwood playscape

68

Children's Farm – starfish vegetable gardens and interactive irrigation ›

Tangshan Quarry Park

Nanjing, Jiangsu Province

Client: Nanjing Tangshan Hot Spring Resort
Type: quarry restoration, public park

Size: 400,000 m²
Year: 2019

Place The 40-hectare site is located at the south of Tangshan National Tourism Resort, an hour's drive from Nanjing, the capital city of Jiangsu province. The former mining area consists of a total of four abandoned quarry sites, distinguished by years of inactivity and geological formation. The giant stone cliffs can be seen from miles away and form a landmark and gateway to Tangshan National Tourism Resort.

Approach Considering the craters to be scars in the landscape, the local government initially intended to remediate the excavation grounds using geoengineering measures. Stunned not only by the gigantic rock formations and mesmerising stone textures, yet also by the vividness of the pioneer vegetation reinhabiting the site, Z+T Studio design acknowledges rather than conceals this dramatic contrast of barren cliffs and burgeoning nature, and establishes a resilient landscape scheme where the derelict mining site can heal in time through natural succession.

Design The management of the water cycle forms the base of Z+T Studio's remediation effort. The terrain was regraded for rainwater harvesting, taking into consideration the varying topography and hydrological conditions of each quarry crater. New meadows were established, and a wetland pond now receives all stormwater run-off from the fields. The former quarry grounds were transformed into four main leisure destinations. The eastern quarry, the deepest and most shielded, serves as a secluded spa area for the resort hotel. The western quarry, which opens up to level fields, functions as an event space and camping ground. The two most spectacular central quarries were converted into a nature exploration park. Corten steel walkways and bridges lead the visitors through the scenery of sharp cliffs and narrow ridges and funnels. Steel nets and erosion control devices reinforce the rock formations

and safeguard the journey through the rugged terrain, from the arc bridge loop at the centre of the crater to the observation deck at the highest point. The walk ends at the playground by the central plain. The playscape features the post-industrial character of the site's origin by employing container modules, hoists and pipes.

Z+T Studio's design addresses the park not only as a destination for eco-learning but as a prototype for future resilient country park design in China, based on long-term prospects and progression rather than short-term revenue gain. In this regard, Z+T Studio's efforts at Nanjing Tangshan Quarry Park encompass an exemplary operational model next to the site design, where multi-level tenants and stakeholders – from the hot spring hotel and restaurants for tourists to music festivals and a camping ground for families and groups – will co-finance the future site management and ongoing remediation measures.

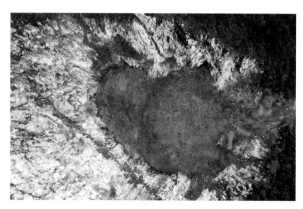

70

Central crater walk – from arc bridge loop to sky deck ››

Before remediation: panorama – pioneer vegetation ‸

Quarry walkway ››

‹ Arc bridge loop

‹ Gabion weirs

‹ Whispering pipes

‹ Container playground

Upper deck ›

Viewing platform ›

Passage of strings ›

Giant trampoline ›

YIYU

Design for the Senses

Shanghai

YIYU
Shanghai

Founder: Lin Yifeng
Founded: 2013
Team: 5–20
Location: Shanghai
Portfolio: public parks and plazas, waterfront design, residential design, museum and exhibition spaces, art installations

YIYU is a boutique landscape architecture studio in Shanghai, founded in 2013 by Lin Yifeng. The studio is nestled in a period mansion in Shanghai's French Concession area. Flower arrangements and in-situ artworks characterise the atmosphere of the small workshop, as YIYU's creative base. The Chinese proverb of 'one world in one flower' holds the key to YIYU's sensory approach to design. The phrase articulates the importance of perception and the interrelationship of the micro- and macrocosms. A flower contains the whole universe; each part of the cosmos reflects the entire cosmos. Perception is the medium for cognition; sensation the essential tool. Revealing the hidden beauty of nature and reinvigorating awareness through design for the senses is the premise of YIYU's creative work, from experimental art to photographic documentaries and project design.

Starting with small scale design interventions and artful floral arrangements, YIYU's portfolio has expanded since the studio's establishment into a wide array of project typologies, ranging from public plaza and residential design to urban waterfront projects and a secluded distillery in the countryside. Close collaborations with leading new architecture practices distinguish YIYU's curated portfolio, allowing each project to challenge established boundaries with experimental design solutions and to create unique loci combining the narratives of the past and the imaginative power of the present.

In conversation with Lin Yifeng about nature's beauty, design for the senses and design collaborations.

After having lived and worked in Boston, New York and Beijing, what made you choose Shanghai as YIYU's studio location?

Lin Yifeng Frankly speaking, I basically immediately felt at home when I arrived in Shanghai seven years ago, and still do today. Shanghai is just a perfect fit for us and our design ambitions and aims, and a great place to meet and collaborate with like-minded international and local creatives. At the same time, Shanghai has changed significantly throughout the past years and for the better, I would say. One simply has to look at all the waterfront rejuvenation projects completed and still in progress.

Lin Yifeng is the Founder and Principal of YIYU. In his creative work, he is committed to a spatial design that interlinks architecture and landscape architecture in favour of an integrated design response, in resonance with nature in its broadest sense and conceptual capacity. Prior to founding YIYU, Lin Yifeng worked at Balmori Associates, New York, and AECOM, Beijing. He is a registered landscape architect in the United States. Lin Yifeng holds a Master of Landscape Architecture from Harvard Graduate School of Design, Cambridge MA, and a Bachelor of Architecture from Tamkang University, Taiwan. In addition to his practise, Lin Yifeng has engaged in academic teaching at the Columbia University Graduate School of Architecture, Planning and Preservation, New York City; Tsinghua University, Beijing; Tongji University, Shanghai; and currently as Adjunct Assistant Professor at Hong Kong University, Shanghai Campus.

‹‹ MOMA waterfront – sky mirrors

Lin Yifeng – YIYU studio – photographic diary ››

Huangpu River has turned from a wasteland to parkland. Suzhou Creek is beginning to develop as a green spine in the city. Adaptive reuse is another topic which has come to the forefront of urban regeneration lately. It's a good place to be and to connect, both locally and internationally.

YIYU's studio is situated in a leafy courtyard in Shanghai's French Concession area – an escape from the city within the city?

Lin Yifeng There's a saying in Chinese: 'a small saint lives in the mountains, yet a true hermit lives in the city'. To me, that perfectly illustrates our studio's thinking and the reason why we chose a location which is in the centre of a big metropolis like Shanghai, but at the same time hidden and secluded. It is the perfect symbiosis of seeming opposites.

As a landscape architecture practice, we are not only concerned about the workplace environment as such but also about our staff's daily route to work. I think it is important to truly understand, experience and value 'green' in the city in your own everyday life before you design this experience for others. Walking past the low-rise townhouses and mansions of the concession area and experiencing the abundance of green and leafy streets on a daily basis is one step on this path.

Also, at our studio space we celebrate green and nature. We share our office space and vision with YIYU's interior design partner. Right from the beginning, when refurbishing the ground floor of the heritage mansion, we were keen to create a studio atmosphere which breaks down the boundaries between the indoor and outdoor environment and recreates a 'sense of nature' throughout. To give an example: we incorporated small trees in the interior studio design and used spotlights to cast the shadow of the trees on the ceiling. Hence now, even when inside we can work 'under a canopy of trees'. Outside in the courtyard, we tend a small nursery where we study plants. 'Testing and doing' is a quintessential part of our studio philosophy. At our workshop room, adjacent to the workstation area, we conduct material studies and experimental works. During the shadow studies for Silhouette Garden, the small room almost turned into a second garden inside.

Coming back to the proverb of the 'small saint versus the true hermit', we see our studio as a hidden workshop, which generates positive energies for the city through landscape design – a place not only for doing and creating but also for thinking, learning and reflecting.

'A small saint lives in the mountains, yet a true hermit lives in the city'.

We see our studio as a hidden workshop, which generates positive energies for the city through landscape design.

Floral artworks decorate the studio, and equally YIYU's project work is often inspired by artful interpretations of nature. Could you share where this derives from?

Lin Yifeng I always thought of landscape as a combination of nature and art. This inspiration has been with me ever since my childhood. I grew up in the countryside in Taiwan. When I was young, we all knew every flower – their scent, the shapes of their leaves, even which parts we could eat. There were rice paddies everywhere, and by observing them we understood the cycle of the seasons. Each season has a different scent in the air, different colours, but also a different usage of the fields. After the harvest, we could fly kites in the fields. This sensitivity about plants inspired me when I was a kid and always stayed with me. I really appreciate nature. Nature doesn't need any designer.

Nature doesn't need a designer?

Lin Yifeng Yes, nature is itself a great designer. What nature creates is already very beautiful and functional at the same time. That's my fundamental belief. A turning point came when I studied architecture, which added another layer of thinking to my basic experience and impression of nature. By comparison, architecture is all about the arranging of either artificial or natural materials, and by doing so creating something new and special. Similarly, one can arrange nature differently or even create something beyond nature. Another influence stems from my mother's work as a professional flower arrangement master. She used all different floral materials, which were already beautiful in their own right, but by organising them differently, a new beauty arose from the composition. A beauty that was not formed by nature itself, but still derived from it. In conclusion, from my point of view, there is no gain to be had in mimicking or reproducing nature. The true challenge is to create an alternative nature.

Could you elaborate what you mean by creating an alternative nature – inventing a second nature or distilling the core beauty of nature?

Lin Yifeng It is about discovering a 'different' beauty 'out' of nature. Take for example some common plants or flowers, which one usually wouldn't

Yes, nature is itself a great designer. What nature creates is already very beautiful and functional at the same time.

There is no gain to be had in mimicking or reproducing nature. The true challenge is to create an alternative nature.

find special or beautiful. Especially in Japanese flower arrangements, masters often use wildflowers or quite ordinary flowers. But by arranging them in contrast of shape or structure or colour tones, something new occurs that wouldn't happen in nature. That is why it is related to art. It is like a painting; we have all the colours created by nature, but only an artist knows how to use them to create a different beauty.

Taiwan in particular is influenced by Japanese culture and design. How do you see yourself as a designer in Asia?

Lin Yifeng My mother already used to combine different floral styles in her arrangements, Western as well as Japanese or other Asian styles. I grew up in Asia but did my master's degree in the United States. I never liked to define which style is what. Style is not important to me. It is far more important *how* to create something that really touches people and evokes an inner emotion or inspiration in the observer. That is why I am interested in art, beauty and nature. There are endless possibilities to recreate something both touching and powerful, innovative and inspiring. But it is also a very delicate task. Take the 'new nostalgia' in recent Chinese residential landscape design, for example. These projects often only scratch the surface of traditional Chinese garden art, like using the most common metaphors. When walking through those landscapes, one won't feel anything. The design is too literal. They are empty – empty of essence. Traditional Chinese garden art at its core is an exquisitely sculpted sequence of experiences which entice the visitors to appreciate nature. For example, there might be a covered path with openings or windows to frame different views onto trees or canopies and to break the boundaries between the indoor and outdoor: walking sheltered yet hearing the sound of the rain. Such experiences define the beauty of traditional gardens. But often this delicacy in the crafting of garden scenes became lost in the transition from traditional garden art to contemporary landscape design – and with it, meaning and magic.

How to create 'meaning' in design? In YIYU's designs you often refer to the term 'design for the senses'.

Lin Yifeng Exactly. You could also call it design for experience. I remember once when I was young, we had gathered for a family dinner when a

Style is not important to me. It is far more important how to create something that really touches people and evokes an inner emotion or inspiration in the observer.

Traditional Chinese garden art at its core is an exquisitely sculpted sequence of experiences, which entice the visitors to appreciate nature.

'Everyone deserves a garden' – photographic documentary of green in the city and people's desire to be close to nature ⌃

tropical rainstorm was brewing outside. I was so stunned by the sound of the rain and its splashing on the ground that I put down my chopsticks, opened an umbrella and walked outside, standing in the rain and simply enjoying the splendour of nature's play. This fundamental touch of nature gave me a sense of what landscape design can do. Our designs can bring hope or romance, excitement or calmness, or even healing to the people. At YIYU, we seek to address and convey this fundamental power of nature in our design, rather than only design something functional, rational or literal. At Silhouette Garden for example, we carefully studied the very shape of flowers and plants, but we didn't arrange them as they would be in a natural environment. Instead, we reconfigured them in an artistic way, almost like a painting. Today, when people enter the garden, they feel as if being immersed into a natural painting crafted by flowers. It is not pure nature. There's a moment of surprise and disruption, and we believe it is this fragile initial moment which evokes awareness and reconnects people with their senses. We do not design *for* the senses in terms of literally encouraging people to smell or touch anything concretely. Instead, we see our designs as toolkits to aid people in rediscovering their inner sensory vocabulary and to encourage everyone to re-engage in sensorial experiences, whether designed or created by nature itself.

We see our designs as toolkits to aid people in rediscovering their inner sensory vocabulary and to encourage everyone to re-engage in sensorial experiences, whether designed or created by nature itself.

How would you define nature as an experience in the city?

Lin Yifeng That's a big topic. But also a very casual one. In our photo documentary, I capture moments of nature in the city in Shanghai but also around the globe on my travels. In Shanghai for example, there was an abandoned piano left out on the street which people used as a flower container. The small balconies in high-density urban districts are another example of 'instant nature'. Too tiny to be really occupied, tenants often turn them into 'vertical gardens'. People are very creative. Another photo I took shows a security guard booth at night with an illuminated goldfish bowl enlivening the place. We believe everyone has an inner desire for nature, and people deserve to find this 'sanctuary' and moment of reconnecting with their senses wherever they live. That's why the series is called 'Everyone deserves a Garden'. For now, it's an initial documentary, but in the future we might develop it into a series of small tools for playing with sunlight, as we did at the Shower of Lights for a public square, on a miniature scale for everyone's home. A Garden of Light for everyone.

'Everyone deserves a garden' – We believe everyone has an inner desire for nature, and people deserve to find this 'sanctuary' and moment of reconnecting with their senses wherever they live.

How is this intent of 'nature for everyone' realised in your projects?

Lin Yifeng One of our greatest advantages is that we work with like-minded architects. At the MOMA waterfront project, we collaborated with Atelier Deshaus architects. From the very beginning, our shared aim was to preserve both types of nature on site, the 'raw architectural nature' of the coal bunker and the naturally grown forest surrounding it.
Another project under construction right now with Neri & Hu architects is the Pernod Ricard malt whiskey distillery at the foothills of Mount Emei, one of the Four Sacred Buddhist Mountains of China. The natural landscape of the project site is incredibly beautiful and pristine – an isolated headland surrounded by a river bend. Often, we find the cue for our design in the landscape itself. In this case, it was the boulders. The architectural vision was to blend the buildings into the landscape. The tasting experience plaza and halls are designed to be partially submerged in the ground. When excavating the basement of this area, a rock layer became exposed. We collected over 150 boulders and integrated them into our site design. The site works required to retrieve the boulders and rearrange them in our landscape design was massive. But the result appears natural and unobtrusive – no scars in the landscape, no nature-defying modernist design, but a fine new landscape accentuated by natural elements which have always been there, yet hidden for the longest time. In the end, our vision in all our projects is to ensure nature remains unharmed and its beauty is revealed to future visitors.

How vital do you consider the collaboration with architects to the success of YIYU's designs?

Lin Yifeng It is critical to our work as it takes the synergy of both disciplines to create a coherent and immersive environment. Also with clients, the owner of Phaedo, with whom we realised Silhouette Garden, utilises all-natural fibres, textures and dyes in his fashion collection. When collaborating on the showroom garden these subtle observations and mutual appreciation of the delicacy of nature were already there. We literally planted the garden together, with our own hands. Every season we visit the garden to see how the original composition has changed and if we should interfere into nature's cycle or not. It has become a very special place for both of us.

Our vision in all our projects is to ensure nature remains unharmed and its beauty is revealed to future visitors.

Silhouette Garden

Shanghai, Xuhui District

Client: Phaedo Studio
Type: showroom garden

Size: 35 m²
Year: 2017

Place Silhouette Garden is located in the French Concession area in Shanghai, a popular inner-city district known for its tree-lined streets, restored heritage mansions and trendy restaurants, cafés and boutique-style retail. As with most of the former concession areas in China, the French quarter, which had been under colonial rule for almost one hundred years from 1849 to 1943, shows the typical blend of Eastern and Western influences in architectural style and building layouts. European-style gated front yards line the leafy streets, while the mansions' inner plans adopted the communal courtyard model of Shanghai's traditional Lilong housing. Silhouette Garden is a courtyard renovation project of Phaedo's newest fashion showroom. The layout of the refurbished, modestly sized mansion is a classic example of the mixed open-space typology in the French Concession area, with a garden in the centre of the residence and a walled forecourt towards the street.

Approach For the appointment-only flagship store serving discerning Shanghai fashionistas, the owner of Phaedo commissioned like-minded creatives in architecture and landscape design to project a corresponding interior and exterior gallery environment, reflecting the core values of the fashion brand through a sensuous and meticulously crafted design. The White Gallery and the Red Teahouse now frame the tiny, 20-square-metre garden, which leads visitors into a world of repose and contemplation.

Though small in physical size, the metaphorical dimensions of the garden reach far beyond its perimeter limits, amplifying the notion of nature in the city. In the words of YIYU: "A garden, as hortus conclusus, is usually defined as an enclosed outdoor space with natural elements in their physical definition. Nonetheless, mentally, a garden is more than a space but a place which reminds us of the awareness of nature, the perception of time, and the emotional linkage to memory: waiting for a flower to bloom, watching a tree grow, observing ivy leaves turn amber. Within a garden, the power of plants is all but strengthened through enclosure and the emphasis on shadow, light, and time."

Design The design strategy of the Silhouette Garden is derived from the concept of a choreographed wilderness reoccupying the space. An assortment of plants, native to Shanghai, was assembled and arranged either in contrast or harmony to each other in the garden; continuously varying the initial composition through growth, blossom, death, and rebirth in time and projecting an ever-changing mural of nature's beauty and expression against the clay perimeter walls.

A series of research experiments preceded the garden design. In the first instance, the Flower Room was installed at the studio workshop. Here, local perennial and aquatic species, which are more adaptable to the garden's humid microclimate, were collected and studied in their colour variations and shape. As part of the Flower Room, the Shadow Curtain was implemented in order to visualise the silhouettes of the plants. During the shadow studies, each species' unique silhouette was traced then catalogued and complementary effects of potential plant arrangements were tested and refined. Lastly, the Crystal Flower series – a three-dimensional artwork by Lin Yifeng, capturing the leaves, seeds and flowers as a sculptural still – concluded the in-house studies.

In spring 2017, Silhouette Garden was jointly built by the design team and the owner of Phaedo Gallery, reconnecting with the nature of the garden. As Lin Yifeng describes the essence of their shared planting effort: "The bond with a plant you plant, the bond with a seed you sow, the longing for a flower to bloom: bonding through self-engagement creates a deeper connection between us humans and nature. And that is what a garden is ultimately all about."

Silhouette studies – depictions of change throughout the cycle of seasons ⌄ ››

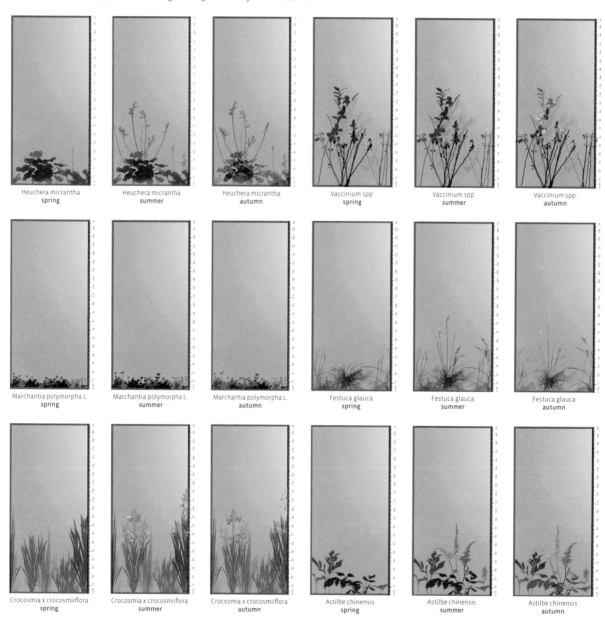

Heuchera micrantha
spring

Heuchera micrantha
summer

Heuchera micrantha
autumn

Vaccinium spp.
spring

Vaccinium spp.
summer

Vaccinium spp.
autumn

Marchantia polymorpha L.
spring

Marchantia polymorpha L.
summer

Marchantia polymorpha L.
autumn

Festuca glauca
spring

Festuca glauca
summer

Festuca glauca
autumn

Crocosmia x crocosmiiflora
spring

Crocosmia x crocosmiiflora
summer

Crocosmia x crocosmiiflora
autumn

Astilbe chinensis
spring

Astilbe chinensis
summer

Astilbe chinensis
autumn

Penstemon campanulatus
spring

Penstemon campanulatus
summer

Penstemon campanulatus
autumn

Acanthus mollis
spring

Acanthus mollis
summer

Acanthus mollis
autumn

‹ White Gallery ››

‹ Red Teahouse ››

‹ Shadow play ››

AVIC Park

Nanchang, Jiangxi Province

Client: AVIC INTL Co. Ltd.
Type: plaza design, villa park, playground
Size: 15,000 m²
Year: 2016

Place AVIC Park is situated in the former Hongdu industrial zone in Qingyunpu district in Nanchang, the capital and largest city of Jiangxi province in south-eastern China. Since its founding in 1951, Hongdu Aviation Industry Group, one of the main military aircraft manufacturers and suppliers in China and a subsidiary of the Aviation Industry Corporation of China (AVIC), had used Qingyunpu Airport for test flights. With the expansion of the city of Nanchang, Qingyunpu Airport became increasingly encircled by residential quarters. With air traffic restricting the district's development, in 2009 Jiangxi provincial government reached an agreement with AVIC to relocate the military airport. In 2013 the former airfield and industrial zone was designated as a new urban development area. At the start of the property redevelopment, two deserted warehouse buildings still marked the entrance to the site, while the former factory grounds were overgrown by a forest of pines.

Approach YIYU defines AVIC Park as a 'timeless habitat' where memory and imagination seamlessly unite. This narrative approach guided YIYU's design interventions when transforming the abandoned industrial site into a new neighbourhood park. Redefined post-industrial scenes now mitigate between the factory remains and the naturally grown forest, taming the wild and integrating the relics and tales of the past into a sustainable park of today.
"What can adaptive reuse mean for Hongdu?
What can urban renewal mean for Nanchang?
A memorial and reflection of our heritage.
An imaginative place for a life full of new possibilities."

Design A Bridge in the Sky, A Valley of Clouds – The former warehouses are converted by Urbanus Architects into office spaces and an exhibition hall, housing Hongdu's aviation retrospective. The landscape design of the entrance plaza equally refers to the site's aviation past.

Pavement resembling folded paper gliders, a favourite local toy, captures the spirit of flying. Stitched paving planes define the ground, rising up to folding timber platforms surrounded by water jets playfully mimicking aircraft engines and condensation trails. Continuing the allegory of flying, a derelict transport link was refurbished into the Bridge in the Sky. Hovering above the terrain, the bridge is the best vantage point for observing the park. From here one overlooks the playground, accentuated by colourful contour lines and animated by timed vapour streams at various intervals: the Valley of Clouds.

Memories of Ancient Trees, Melodies of the Wind – Within the park area, the protection of the existing mature pines became the defining task of the site design. YIYU considers the preservation of memory and sustainable renewal to be intrinsically connected: "Every tree is a witness to Hongdu's history, an important keeper of memory, as well as a guardian of the land." All trees on site were preserved, and the path system aligned with minimal impact to the forest. At the entrance to the park, a raised timber platform is inserted into the woods to create a stage under the canopies; a place for the neighbourhood to gather in the cooling shade and listen to the sound of the breeze through the leaves: the Melodies of the Wind.

Living in the Woods, Hiding in the Wild – Three display villas are integrated into the forested area of the site. The villas are carefully placed among the trees. Partially clad with polished stainless steel, the future homes reflect the greens of the leaves and seamlessly blend into the forest environment.

The naturally grown wood primarily consists of pines, mixed with camphor, golden rain and citrus trees. The canopies are trimmed to improve the light conditions of the understorey and to allow the shrub layer to recuperate. Rainwater is collected in dry creeks and retention ponds and reused for site irrigation.

AVIC forest – Living in the Woods – Hiding in the Wild ››

Valley of Clouds playscape – contour-coloured topography suffused in clouds of mist at intervals ∨ ››

< Forest plaza

< Exhibition hall

< Light clouds

Aviation plaza >

Seed displays >

Shower of Light
Nanchang, Jiangxi Province

Client: Greenland Holdings Corp. Ltd.
Type: art installation, plaza design

Size: 800 m²
Year: 2018

Place The project forms part of Nanchang's Rule district development. The city extension area, in the early stages of urban development, appears non-descript and lacks identity. Suitable public urban spaces for early and future residents are sparse. The notion of nature is absent, as is the liveliness of established city districts.

Approach Confronted with the vagueness in identity and character and the absence of contextual references, YIYU opted for a standalone artistic intervention, to enliven the place: the Shower of Lights.

Design The Shower of Lights capitalises on sunlight as the area's most powerful natural element. With an average of nearly two thousand hours of sunshine per year in Nanchang, peaking in summer and autumn with five to nine hours a day, the idea was born to make the play of sunlight become nature's agent – activating the space and counterbalancing its barrenness.

Taking the ease and unpredictability of butterflies fluttering in gardens and filling the space with colour and life as a source of inspiration, the designers created a semi-transparent canopy of close to a thousand colourful acrylic glass panels suspended above the square. Bright red, purple and green were chosen as the colour tones of the butterfly panels and tested in-house to define the colour distribution and arrangement across the suspension screen.

In order to minimise side effects and interference in the shadow play of the panels through structural components, preference was given to a lightweight steel cable mesh affixed to a frame of thin perimeter columns. The cable net structure gently flexes between the anchor points, creating the natural shape of the canopy and the subtle distortion and overlay of colourful shadows cast by the rigid grid of acrylic glass butterflies.

"When sunlight passes through the canopy, the light transforms into a thousand colourful butterflies on the ground and creates a bath of lights in the space. A place where kids can blend into the lights, chase shadows and play with nature. The contrasting colour design of the acrylic panels converts the sunlight normally less perceptible into something noticeable, vivid and beautiful, creating dynamic moving colours that bridge the gap between users and nature," summarises Lin Yifeng about the attributes of YIYU's installation, concluding: "By uniting nature and users, the landscape has become the new identity of the place."

I've watched you now a full half-hour;
Self-poised upon that yellow flower
And, little Butterfly! indeed
I know not if you sleep or feed.
How motionless!

and ...

Shower of Lights – butterfly canopy ››

Concept – poem by William Wordsworth (1770–1850) ^

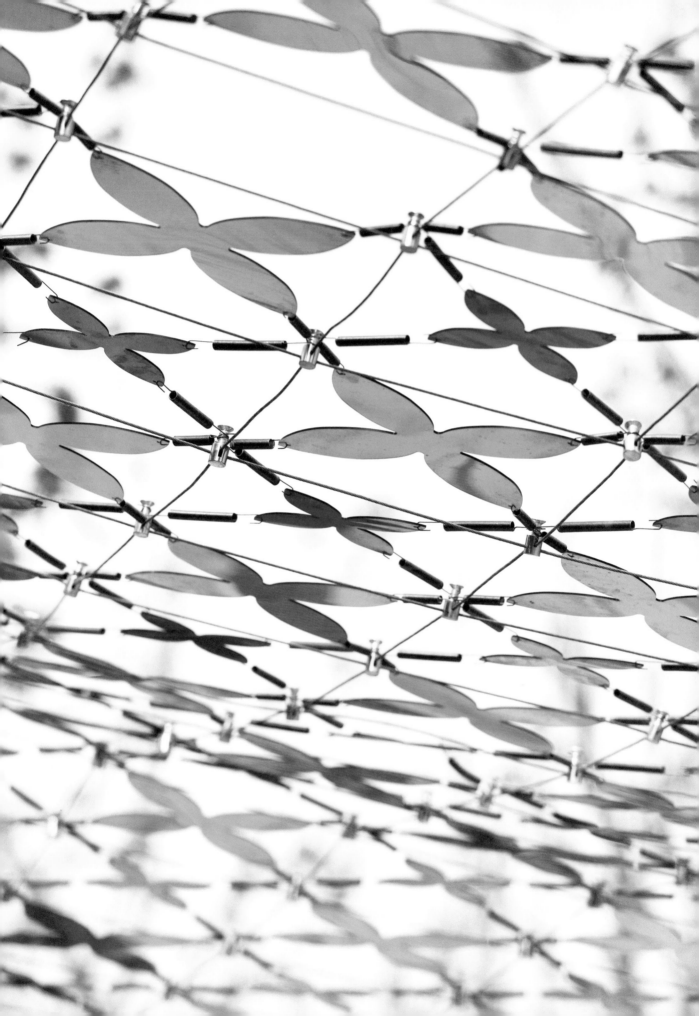

Shadow studies

Overlay of colours

acrylic panel

200 mm   100 mm

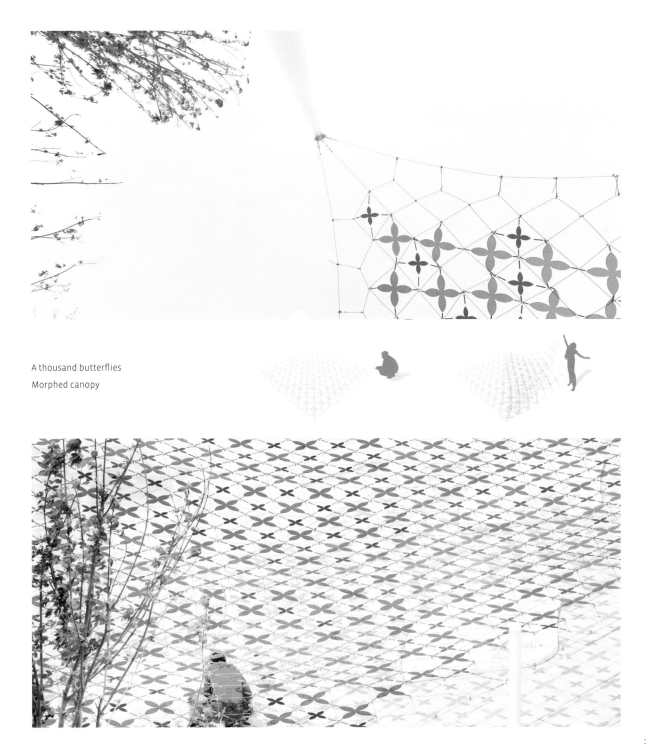

A thousand butterflies
Morphed canopy

Gallery of Nature
Suzhou, Jiangsu Province

Client: AVIC INTL; Poly Property Group Co. Ltd.
Type: residential design

Size: 4,800 m²
Year: 2019

Place Suzhou is home to over sixty classical Chinese gardens, collectively recognised as a UNESCO World Heritage site. The Humble Administrator's Garden and the Lingering Garden in Suzhou's Old Town are among the four most renowned classical gardens in China. Recapturing the beauty of nature in miniature landscape scenes is essential to Chinese garden art. To achieve these exquisitely detailed frames of nature, bonsai gardening techniques developed across China, with Suzhou-style bonsai legendary for its long history, unique design and distinctive style, unparalleled in its minimalist pureness and elegance.

Approach YIYU's design for the new residential compound addresses both the historical attributes of Suzhou's famous private residences and the layout principles of residential compounds today. By reinterpreting traditional techniques, the design seeks to transform classical garden scenes into modern landscape frames, accommodating present rituals of inhabitation of open space. Taking the bonsai gardening school of Suzhou as a cue, the design of the Gallery of Nature applies a reversed approach: designing miniature bonsai scenes and re-enlarging them into real-scale design; creating 'blow-up' miniature gardens, as YIYU terms the planting design strategy at Gallery of Nature.

Design The entrance gate in vernacular Chinese architecture traditionally operates as a functional as well as symbolic divide, shielding the privacy of the residences from the outside world. In YIYU's design the traditional Chinese gate structure is redefined as an open shared space, mitigating between privacy and publicness and inviting residents as well as neighbouring communities to gather and socialise. The covered walkway, which replaced the walled gate along the perimeter of the property, denotes the open character of the entrance to the compound. Stone walls intersecting the

walkway segment the view along the walk into a series of perspectives onto the garden.

Next in the sequence from public to semi-public is the water garden. The yard is composed of several garden islets with local deciduous and fruit trees, ornamental grasses and aquatic plants, capturing the beauty of the seasons in Suzhou in selected frames. The refined plant arrangements apply the same techniques as traditional bonsai displays, yet reverse the process from condensing nature into miniature compositions – to be experienced visually only – into original scale planting frames, to be explored spatially throughout the seasons.

A community library and café with outdoor terrace line the water garden and link the interior and exterior residential environments. The swimming pool forms the centre of the communal areas of the compound. Coloured tiles evoke the illusion of an emerald lake where users can float among colours, enwrapped in the reflection of the sky. Bamboo screens and mist fountains provide shade and cooling in summer, further blurring the contrast of the elements.

"A dreamlike place is created by sequential sensuous experiences, and poetic imagination is amplified into a fantasy of water living. The project redefines the concept of gated residences, both in history and in the gated communities of today. We believe a garden shared by everyone and designed in resonance of culture and nature, can provide a sustainable model for future residential developments."

Courtyard pool – floating among colours and reflections ››

Water garden – bonsai blow-up garden islets ᴧ

MOMA Waterfront

Shanghai, East Bund

Client: Shanghai Bund Investment Group Ltd.
Type: waterfront design

Size: 42,000 m²
Year: 2017

Place The MOMA waterfront park is located on the East Bund of Huangpu River, a tributary of the Yangtze River that extends to the East China Sea. Throughout history, the waterway has been a significant engine in the city's rapid development. From the late nineteenth to the early twentieth century, the shipyards, factories, and warehouses at the riverbanks fuelled Shanghai's transformation from a sleepy backwater town into a vibrant trading hub. The beginning of the new millennium marked a turning point for Shanghai's economy, as the city moved from secondary to tertiary industries. As such, it became the moment in time for local government to reconsider the river's role within the city. The transformation plan of the riverfront from industrial site to public greenway was established and listed in the city's development plans for 1999–2020 and reinforced in the three-year action plan for Huangpu waterfront redevelopment from 2015 to 2017. Docks and warehouses from the past were removed or converted into museums and exhibition halls, while riverside parks and walking trails were built to reconnect the riverfront with the urban fabric of the city. By the end of 2017, 45 kilometres of the Huangpu waterfront had been opened to the public, and an array of new museums had turned the river into the cultural artery of Shanghai. The transformation of the Laobaidu coal bunker into the Museum of Modern Art (MOMA) by Atelier Deshaus and the waterfront park by YIYU was one of the key projects of this ambitious urban rejuvenation initiative.

Approach Preserving the unique character of the industrial remains, while adapting them to new functions and making them accessible to the public, became the most prominent challenge for the architecture as well as the landscape architecture design. Working closely together, the designers of Atelier Deshaus and YIYU concluded not only to preserve the bunker building but also its exterior extensions and the natural environment, which had taken over the site during its years of abandonment. Inside the museum, the raw industrial interior is largely preserved, creating a dramatic shell for the exhibits. Outdoors, the crude concrete framework of the former coal feeders was kept and reused as the support structure for the elevated walkway and industrial hull of the glass facades of the cafés and community facilities below.

Design The Beauty of Nature and Time – The new entry plaza of the museum connects the waterfront with the exhibition areas and the skywalk above. To echo the site's coal processing history, the paving utilises terrazzo techniques, integrating recycled stones from the site to reflect the industrial character and texture of the place. The grove of camphor and Chinese tallow trees adjacent to the former coal bunker was maintained. Seasonal meadows and native grasses create a field of nature in the city, additionally enhancing the contrast of time. Above, the skywalk invites the visitors to journey through the canopies of the trees, providing striking views of the linear park and the skyline of the city. The walkway ends at the reflecting pool at the southern edge of the site, mirroring the sky and the change of colours through the seasons.

Nature in the city – raw industrial relics – translucent new amenities ››

MOMA waterfront – landscape masterplan ˄

Sky bridge and reflection pool ∧

< From ground to sky

^ Sky mirrors and perennial fields

From sky to ground ›

Moshang

Comfort and Tradition

Shanghai

Moshang
Shanghai

Founder: Chen Xiaoli, Ke Lijuan
Founded: 2011
Team: 5–20
Location: Shanghai
Portfolio: exterior decoration, outdoor furniture design, artworks, show garden fittings, material sampling and sourcing

Moshang is an exterior design company established in 2011 by Chen Xiaoli and Ke Lijuan in Shanghai. With their professional background in landscape design management at a top-tier property development company in China, Chen Xiaoli and Ke Lijuan realised that there was a missing link in all projects: the final soft fittings. While the landscape design throughout the projects was custom-designed and site-specific, the outdoor furniture design was lacking the same attention to detail and professionalism in product design and manufacturing. Hence, the idea behind Moshang was born: a specialised landscape practice focusing exclusively on exterior decoration, expanding the established landscape design portfolio and offering end-user outdoor lifestyle experience and leisure design. Starting from a niche market, Moshang's portfolio has grown to encompass a wide array of furniture design lines and artworks across China.

International furniture design trends, innovative materials and production methods inspire Moshang's work, along with local ingenuity and crafts. Their exterior decorations add the final touch to residential landscapes. Custom-made and tailored to the project specifics, Moshang's outdoor furniture and sculptures provide comfort and add depth and meaning to the residences, on an experiential as well as on a metaphorical level. Thus, closing a second missing link: a modern outdoor environment, fitting the worldliness of Chinese urbanities while being authentic and referential to local traditions.

Chen Xiaoli is the Co-founder and Director of Moshang and oversees the design development and operational management of the studio. Her expertise in both design and implementation ensures consistency in the execution and quality of all prototype furniture design. Prior to founding Moshang, Chen Xiaoli worked at the Landscape and Park Management Department of Shanghai's Luwan district and led the Landscape Design Management Department at Shanghai Vanke Real Estate Development. She is the co-author of the Green Book in 2007, a practice manual for landscape architecture design and construction. Chen Xiaoli holds a Bachelor of Landscape Architecture from China Northeast Forestry University, Harbin.

Ke Lijuan is the Co-founder and Design Director of Moshang and leads the creative process of the studio. Inspired by traditional Chinese iconography and arts as well as international furniture design, Ke Lijuan creates the modern yet authentic look of all artworks and furniture lines of the studio. Prior to founding Moshang, Ke Lijuan worked at Vanke Real Estate Development in Tianjin and Shanghai. She recorded the cultural preservation and site renewal of Crystal City at ABBS, China Architectural Design Forum, and co-authored the Green Book in collaboration with Chen Xiaoli. Ke Lijuan holds a Bachelor of Landscape Architecture from Nanjing Forestry University.

In conversation with Ke Lijuan and Chen Xiaoli about exterior design as stage setting, traditional crafts and international suppliers.

How did the idea of Moshang as a studio specialised in exterior decoration come into being?

Chen Xiaoli Lijuan and I have always shared this fascination for outdoor living. At Vanke Real Estate Development, where we worked before, we jointly edited a landscape handbook including an extensive section on outdoor fabrics and furnishing. As design managers, we faced the lack of professionalism in this area on a daily basis. The manual was a first attempt to address this issue.

<< Jinlin Cloud Mansion – ceramic stools

Chen Xiaoli (l.), Ke Lijuan (r.) – Moshang team >>

Ke Lijuan When starting Moshang, we actually discussed at length which term to use to describe our service. Ten years ago, no one else was doing this type of work. It was a completely new sector in the landscape design industry. In the end, we settled on the term 'exterior decoration'. It is an easy to comprehend 'task description'. But what we are really concerned with is different. I would rather call it: setting a stage for a scene.

Chen Xiaoli We are both landscape architects, not product designers. We don't approach our projects from the 'object', like designing a piece of furniture and later simply placing it in a garden or yard. We are interested in creating an entire atmosphere. Our furniture elements are just the 'agents' in place, you could say. Our approach is closer to designing a stage for a theatre play. Our displays create drama through artistry. They nuance and bring forward the character of place. We seek to create an environment to be interpreted and inhabited through our furniture.

Ke Lijuan It is like a theatre stage but in real life. People can live in it and enjoy the space. It is not something to watch only from a distance. It is a creation and reflection of a lifestyle – often an ideal lifestyle.

Moshang's work often references poems as the source of the design. How does this relate to 'setting a stage for a lifestyle'?

Ke Lijuan In our projects, we recreate an atmosphere which 'touches' upon the ideal lifestyle in ancient times, but in a contemporary manner. Chinese tradition is passed on by poems which depict a scene, most often a landscape scene. We are all familiar with those core scenes in literature. We heard them from our parents; we learned about them in school.
For example, there is a scene called Liang Gui Dang Ting. As with most proverbs, it is difficult to translate. Literally, it means: 'Two osmanthus trees in the courtyard.' But the real meaning is only revealed through the interplay of Chinese characters. In Chinese, there are two different characters which both share the similar pronunciation 'Gui'. One means 'osmanthus tree' as in the verse and the other indicates 'high status or importance'. Hence Liang Gui Dang Ting is often used as an auspicious wish in China. Similarly, the poems of Tang dynasty poet Li Bai (701–762), that we referred to at Violet Palace, depict beautiful scenes in life which carry meaning far beyond what is actually described, like Yue Xia Du Zhuo:

We are both landscape architects, not product designers. We are interested in creating an entire atmosphere. Our furniture elements are just the 'agents' in place.

We recreate an atmosphere which 'touches' upon the ideal lifestyle in ancient times but in a contemporary manner.

112

'Drinking alone under the moon, toasting to the moon and the shadow, becoming a party of three.' In everyday life, we usually don't mention these poems, but when one does, the scenes immediately come to mind.

Could you expand on how these poetic scenes you mentioned influence your design thinking and process?

Chen Xiaoli Honestly, that is just how we think. In my mind, the scene always appears first, never the object. The first image contains the atmosphere, and then I begin thinking about any other concrete object in space. Another particularly interesting point is: When we talk with our clients, the moment we mention a certain scene from poetry, everyone knows what we are talking about – and knows on a very deep level, on a level beyond the factual. We do not need to explain any further. It is just shared cultural knowledge. To answer the question: first the scenes and then the artefacts.

Where do you see the connection between ancient poems and modern life in the 21st century?

Ke Lijuan Modern Chinese people still appreciate the ancient dreams of poets and intellectuals. Their lyrical depictions and imaginations are fundamental and timeless, and still the lifestyle we adore. Especially today, with the fast development of the economy and wealth of Chinese citizens, cultural and spiritual wealth has become equally important. The poetry reminds us of these high ethical principles in life which became forgotten in our everyday life and busy schedules. We lost something in the process of economic development. That is why we revive that dream of our ancestors in our designs and give it a tangible modern expression.

How does this approach translate into furniture design?

Chen Xiaoli Take Jinlin Cloud Mansion as an example. It is an interesting project regarding both its relation to the ancient admiration of nature and for the integration of traditional crafts into contemporary furniture design. When we visited the site, there was a sunken green, projected as a music theatre. We were immediately reminded of a verse called Da Zhu Xiao Zhu Luo Yu Pan, written by Bai Juyi during the Tang dynasty.

The moment we mention a certain scene from poetry, everyone knows what we are talking about – and knows on a very deep level, on a level beyond the factual.

Ke Lijuan The verse describes the sound of raindrops. Some droplets are large, and some are tiny. When they fall on the lotus leaves, the leaves will not move. That is the essence of the scene depicted in the poem.

Chen Xiaoli Also, a spectrum of colours will occur when the sunlight is reflected in the water droplets. We choose ceramic to transform these colours and seasonality into a designed object. The various colours of the glaze will show different reflections in sunshine or rain. They will create a kaleidoscope of colours just as it happened in the time of Bai Juyi.

For the ceramic stools and chairs in Jinlin Cloud Mansion, Moshang worked closely with the craftsmen of a nearby kiln. Could you share some insights from the process of fabrication?

Ke Lijuan Jinlin Cloud Mansion is located at Lake Tai. The region is famous for its traditional ceramics. Yixing city, just across the lake, is an important centre of clayware in China. In this respect, the ceramic elements not only resonate with the atmosphere of the garden but also with the identity of place.

Chen Xiaoli We had often worked with this particular kiln before. When the idea of ceramic stools and chairs came up, we knew it would be complicated. But when we approached the owners of the kiln, they were willing to help us make the design happen. Nonetheless, the beginning was a disaster. The first stools cracked or became deformed during the firing process – some even exploded completely. The size was too big; the shape seemed uncontrollable. The colour of the glazing wasn't good either. We spent a long time testing. In the end, we made small holes in each stool, allowing the steam building up inside the 'vessel' to be released during the firing. The other issue was the glazing. The chairs are multi-coloured. Hence, we needed to apply three rounds of glazing to achieve the colouring effect we wanted. But with every new layer, we ran the risk of bursting and cracks forming in the glaze all over again if the temperature was inconsistent.

Ke Lijuan It was a crazy process with many failures and faulty goods. We were extremely lucky to be supported by senior craftsmen – true artists and creative minds ready to take on the 'impossible'.

The verse describes the sound of raindrops. Some droplets are large, and some are tiny. When they fall on the lotus leaves, the leaves will not move. That is the essence of the scene depicted in the poem.

The ceramic elements not only resonate with the atmosphere of the garden but also with the identity of place.

Chungeng, furniture collection – combining Chinese woodwork with soft international outdoor fabrics ⌃

Chen Xiaoli In the ceramic industry, you would usually not do any such large pieces. There were structural problems, as they have no steel structure inside and are completely made by hand. Each piece is a unique signature piece by one of the craftsmen. Also, the final product has problems as ceramic elements are affected by the outdoor temperature, especially during the rainy season. We modelled each chair at least eight to ten times and had to fire around five to achieve one good one without any cracks or unintentional bleeding colours of the glaze. But ultimately, we made it. The stools and chairs are in the garden of Jinlin Mansion, and we kept some 'defective' ones at our private homes.

Ke Lijuan The entire process was carried by the creativity and ingenuity of the craftsmen. A fact we often experience when collaborating with manufacturers or other disciplines. There is an entrepreneurial spirit throughout the industry. We often expand our capabilities together. We absolutely benefitted from the knowledge of the craftsmen, but equally the collaboration provided an opportunity for them to elevate their product palette from traditional household objects to a new and innovative contemporary product line.

Elegant Mansion is another good example of the synergy we seek, in this case in art and design. Here, we worked together with Zhang Zhoujie, an acclaimed digital artist in China. Naturally, he would develop pieces to be exhibited in museums, a protected indoor environment, rather than outdoor sculptures exposed to the weather and human touch. At that stage, he had just begun to question this approach in favour of objects that can really engage with the public beyond the safety of museum grounds. And so, he joined us in the development of the Spinner series.

Moshang works with both national and international suppliers. Do you have a preference for sourcing locally or from abroad?

Chen Xiaoli Most definitely. We make a clear distinction between 'soft' materials such as outdoor fabrics, which we source internationally, and 'hard' materials, including woodworks, metal or ceramic, which we produce locally. The reason being is that upholstered soft outdoor seating is uncommon in China; or at least it was ten years ago when Moshang started. Nowadays it is different, as people experienced luxury outdoor furnishing during their travels abroad and expect to find the

The entire process was carried by the creativity and ingenuity of the craftsmen. There is an entrepreneurial spirit throughout the industry. We often expand our capabilities together.

In our projects, we mix soft fabrics from abroad with 'hardware' done in China. So far, this has proven to be a very successful combination. The 'hard' Chinese furniture can actually become 'soft'.

The creative industry in China, in general, has become more confident. There is a great vibe around in exploring new ways at our own doorstep and in the wider Asian region.

same comfort in public areas of their residential compounds at home, both outdoors and indoors. Traditionally, outdoor furniture in China was made from stone or, depending on the region, occasionally from bamboo or wood. Hence, there was no industry established in China with a proven record of quality outdoor textiles. Outdoor textiles require a higher quality standard than fabrics used inside as they have to be weather resistant, with neither their colours bleaching in sunshine nor the fabrics attracting mould during the rainy season. There is no middle ground for what concerns product quality. When we founded Moshang we started with an American supplier, though nowadays we also work with textile manufacturers from Europe, mainly from Italy, Spain and France.

In our projects, we mix soft fabrics from abroad with 'hardware' done in China. So far, this has proven to be a very successful combination. The 'hard' Chinese furniture can actually become 'soft'. Also, the range of manufacturers available in China is broad and diverse. All our furniture is custom-made. Depending on the type of material and design, we can choose between engaging local craftsmen or using modern laser cutting technologies. Both are still equally accessible in China at affordable rates.

You both travel extensively and are regular visitors to the Milan Furniture Fair. Which new impulses or inspirations do you gather from these trips?

Ke Lijuan It is always great to be in Italy. Ten per cent of the Milan fair is dedicated to outdoor products, which is always interesting and inspiring. Same with Art Basel for impulses from the arts. When Xiaoli and I returned from Italy in 2014, we decided to start our own product line with a Chinese touch. That's how Chungeng came into being in 2019, a subsidiary of Moshang, where we design and manufacture our own furniture lines and collections independent from commissioned projects.

Chen Xiaoli As Lijuan said, it is always inspiring to see new global trends. Nonetheless, I think the days of following or even imitating overseas trends are gone. The creative industry in China, in general, has become more confident. There is a great vibe around in exploring new ways at our own doorstep and in the wider Asian region. Maybe one day we will exhibit our furniture at the Milan Fair – that may be just a distant dream for now, but it is a beautiful one.

Elegant Mansion
Shanghai, Pudong District

Client: Shanghai Westlake Hotel Apartment
Type: exterior decoration, clubhouse

Size: 3,700 m²
Year: 2018

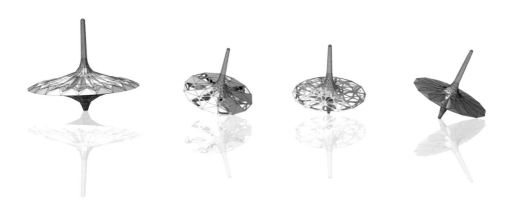

Place Elegant Mansion is a new residential development located in the historic township of Zhoupu in Pudong district, primarily targeted at young professionals and families. Well-educated and worldly through overseas travel or study experience, they represent the typical new Chinese middle class, seeking a high standard of life in their working and living environment.

Approach Whilst the architectural style of the compound follows a strictly contemporary and minimalist approach, the landscape design aims to enrich the site with meaning by creating a minimalist Chinese Mountain Water Garden with tangible objects carrying symbolic connotations.

Design Designing with metaphors is key to Moshang's approach to exterior decoration. Also, at Elegant Mansion, the essential question at the beginning of the project was to determine the right allegory that would speak to the young, urbane future residents in an evocative and multifaceted way.

The Spinner became the parable of choice. Most potential homebuyers, now in their thirties, grew up in the late 1970s to 1980s, when living standards in China were still low and only few toys available. The spinner stands out as a toy from those decades, bringing back memories of joy and simple childhood pleasures. Coinciding with the construction of Elegant Mansion, a new interpretation of the traditional toy was omnipresent in the media: the rotating spinner depicted in the movie Inception as a tool for endless expansion of time and space. This coincidence gave rise to the idea of the Spinner, both as a symbolic representation of childhood memory and of futuristic imagination.

The final design of the Spinner was developed in close collaboration with Zhang Zhoujie, a renowned artist and pioneer in the field of digital creation. The architecture of Elegant Mansion is composed of seven buildings. Equally, the formation of the Spinner is based on the concept of the number 7. In Chinese culture, the number 7 represents the combination of natural science and the humanities. Hence, the Spinner is designed in multiples of '7': the 7 modules of '7*1', the 14 modules of '7*2' and the 21 modules of '7*3'. The precise refraction in proportion and percentage of the spread of the arithmetic modules records the sky, the clouds, the water, buildings, trees and people; in total creating a tangible form through which to 'observe the big through the small'.

The sunken garden inside the compound follows the opposite approach to the Spinner. Here, a 'small area contains the big world'. The garden is designed as a meditation space and miniature landscape. All outdoor furniture design by Moshang derives from natural material and shapes. Wood is cut into soft curves, resembling rocks eroded by a stream of water. Sitting or lying down on the soft curves of the long bench and watching the sky, one feels transported back in time, away from the city, towards the tranquillity of a mountain forest. The design of the garden invites the visitors to discover the whole world within a small garden through the creation of objects, which is the essence of traditional Chinese landscape gardens.

‹ Sunken garden ››
‹ Floating bench ››

Lake Mansion
Suzhou, Jiangsu Province

Client: Suzhou Xuyue Property Co Ltd
Type: exterior decoration, clubhouse

Size: 11,000 m²
Year: 2016

Place Suzhou is a unique and culturally rich historic city renowned for its classical Chinese gardens, dating from the Northern Song to the late Qing dynasties (11th–19th centuries) and for its well-preserved old town, where the classic layout of traditional Chinese water towns still prevails today. Elegant Mansion is situated at the lakeside of Dushu Lake within the Higher Education District of Suzhou Industrial Park (SIP). The relationship to the surrounding waters is revived by an outdoor environment resembling the atmosphere of the South of the Yangtze River Water Towns.

Approach The design of the outdoor furniture demonstrates a hybrid of traditional culture, contemporary aesthetics and artistic interventions, collectively shaping a modern-day living and leisure environment. In order to create a vivid and varied outdoor experience, the designers refrained from choosing any one singular traditional pattern or icon as leading decorative motif. Instead, they reintroduced a collection of traditional, almost forgotten household objects from the South of the Yangtze River Water Towns, reinterpreted as contemporary leisure furniture for the courtyard: the four-poster bed with canopy; the bamboo basket full of snacks; the square table for family gatherings; the bamboo chair and vintage reclining chair for laid-back summer evenings.

Design The daybed at the garden pool is inspired by the traditional Chinese four-poster bed. Slender stainless steel columns frame the daybed. The original palm fibre mattress of the bed is replaced by a thin plate of single custom-made ceramic tiles. Due to the traditional hand-colouring technique applied, each tile shows a unique and unpredictable gradation of indigo after firing in the kiln. Dispersed across the surface of the daybed, a special effect occurred: the assemblage of indigos resembled a traditional Chinese water ink painting, depicting the subtle ripples of Dushu Lake.

The daybed, as well as the bamboo chair and reclining chair, can be easily moved within the clubhouse atrium, allowing for the leisure areas to be rearranged depending on the season or time of day.

The Four-Directions Sofa completes the collection. Its layout stems from the traditional household square table, where family members for centuries came together from all directions to chat, play and enjoy home-cooked food. The Four-Directions Sofa shares this intention. It is custom-made for the terrace area of the clubhouse, a casual meeting place for friends and strangers alike. In line with the daybed in the courtyard, the frame of the sofa is built of stainless steel square tubes. The sofa is divided into four seating segments, each facing a different direction. Four upholstered seat cushions provide comfort. They are covered with top quality faux leather fabric for durability and distinction. Although inspired by traditional furniture, the sofa adopts a neutral modern style. Through the contrast of slenderness and solidity, the combination of hardness and softness and the matching colours of indigo and bronze, the sofa reinvigorates the spatial atmosphere of the South of the Yangtze River Water Towns, creating a seating space for future residents to relax and unwind.

122

Daybed – reinterpreting the traditional Chinese four-poster bed ^

Clubhouse terrace – lounge furniture collection ››
Pool area – daybed and reclining chair collection ››

Royal Garden
Shanghai, Pudong District

Client: Hongshida Real Estate Development
Type: exterior decoration, clubhouse

Size: 11,000 m²
Year: 2016

Place Royal Garden is a neoclassical Chinese-style residential compound located in Huinan town, a suburb of Shanghai. The new development caters to China's new middle class with high expectations of quality of life, regarding both comfort and cultural identity.

Approach Never since the Six Dynasties (222–589 CE), have Chinese people ceased their longing for the life described by the poet Tao Yuanming (365–427 CE) in his famous fable of an ethereal land, where people lead an ideal existence in harmony with nature, unaware of the outside world, called the Peach Blossom Spring (Tao Hua Yuan). The expression Tao Hua Yuan has since become the standard Chinese term for 'utopia'.
Shanghai's annual Peach Blossom Festival is held in Huinan town, in the vicinity of Royal Garden. Moshang's peach tree sculpture at the forecourt of the new residences pays tribute to both the present-day festival and Tao Yuanming's masterpiece of a utopian world.

Design Two peach trees form the centrepieces of the arrival courtyard, one artificial and one natural. The two peach trees play on the dichotomy between nature and art. The natural tree will grow freely and change its form and appearance throughout the seasons and years, while the artificial tree will remain unaltered in its original state, frozen in time. The trees are placed diagonally to each other, emphasising the dialogue of different natures within one space.
In contrast to the natural tree, Moshang's artistic peach tree interpretation minimises the visual impact of the trunk and branches and puts the spotlight on the wind in the leaves. When implementing the vision, the structural design of the artificial tree became the core concern, when seeking to achieve a stable structure without compromising the delicate nature of the tree. The solution was a structural skeleton of steel bars that frame the tree and allow the shiny gold-plated leaves to

freely flutter in the breeze, attracting the attention of the visitors and seemingly bringing the artificial tree to life. Yu Shu Lin Feng is the name of the installation, given to it by the client when he first saw the realised artwork on site. The poetic Chinese idiom describes 'a beautiful tree which looks like a handsome gentleman, standing in the wind, with a breeze blowing his robe in the air'. The phrase not only portrays the interplay between the natural tree, the artificial tree and the forces of the wind but also symbolises the courtesy and warm welcome offered to future residents and guests.

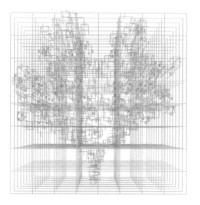

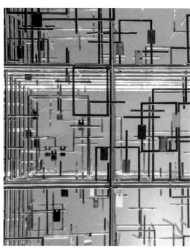

Forecourt – dialogue between natural and artificial tree ››

Structural frame – moving gold-plated leaves ︿

Jinlin Cloud Mansion

Suzhou, Jiangsu Province

Client: New Hope Real Estate Co. Ltd.
Type: exterior decoration, residential design

Size: 7200 m²
Year: 2019

Place Jinlin Cloud Mansion is located in Wujiang district, Suzhou, in close proximity to Lake Tai, one of the sites where the history and culture of Jiang Nan – meaning south of the Yangtze River – originated. The positioning of the project as a modern living place of Jiang Nan responds to this local connotation.

Approach In tune with the vivid graphical layout of the garden design by EcoLand, Shanghai, Moshang's exterior decoration seeks to further boost the experience of the users through evocative furniture design.

Design The U-shaped atrium and garden are interpreted as the Butterfly Garden. In response to the paving pattern referencing the wings of butterflies, Moshang designed a 360-degree view, winding bench for the garden terrace. The curvilinear seating element maximises the viewing angles and denotes different seating sections, creating niches for groups and families to gather along the bench. The table top around a tree marks the end of the elongated bench.

Colourful ceramic stairs and stools are the highlight of the garden. The ancient Chinese had already discovered the outstanding durability of ceramics in outdoor environments. Garden tables and chairs were decorated with ceramic plates depicting ideal landscapes of mountains and rivers, and flowers and birds. In the outdoor furniture line for Jinlin Cloud Mansion, Moshang borrows from these traditional crafts and reinvents outdoor ceramic elements in a modern interpretation. Red and blue are the leading colour tones of the glaze, as in traditional Chinese porcelain. The final flow effect of the modern glazing is achieved by a three-stage firing process in the kiln. Each ceramic chair is unique and made by a different craftsman of the workshop. The distinct characteristics of each piece of the collection not only stem from each master's craft applied in the process of shaping, but also from the duration and level

of heat during the firing. Exposed to wind and rain, the ceramic chairs always look bright and shiny, yet never glare in sunlight.

The Lotus Pond Theatre complements the Butterfly Garden as a casual meeting area for the residents. The custom-made ceramic stools depict morning dew on lotus leaves. Naturally scattered across the lawn, they appear like outlandish plants mushrooming in the grass and invite the residents to sit or lean on them and to most unconditionally and intuitively inhabit the space.

Jinlin Cloud Mansion – concept illustration ››

Butterfly Garden and curvilinear bench ˄

Ceramic chairs ›
Butterfly Garden

‹‹ Ceramic stools
Lotus Pond Theatre

Rong Garden

Shanghai, Jing'an District Shanghai

Client: Financial Street Holding Co. Ltd.
Type: exterior decoration, clubhouse

Size: 22,600 m²
Year: 2018

Place Rong Garden is situated in close vicinity to Shanghai Railway Station in Jing'an district. As the first phase of the residential quarters of Shanghai Financial Street, a multi-building mixed-use complex, Rong Garden is a showcase of the city centre's new lifestyle in Shanghai. The architecture design of the project revisits Shanghai's art deco heritage, branding the development as a new heritage-style landmark of the city.

Approach The target clientele of Rong Garden is China's middle-class professionals. Financially successful, they crave essence and meaning beyond physical comfort in their living environment. Creating a community space that fosters a calm and relaxing experience within the thriving urban centre of Shanghai became the maxim of Moshang's outdoor furniture design.

Design Moshang believes that materials are the soul of outdoor furniture. At Rong Garden, timber is the leading material and the means of expression of the courtyard's atmosphere. Gold silk teak wood, commonly used in traditional Chinese indoor furniture, became the material of choice for all outdoor furniture at Rong Garden.

The design of the community area is divided into five spaces: the Living Room, Nature Park, Water Garden, Star Garden and Children's Playground. The Living Room forms the core area of the community. Here, two elongated benches take centre stage. Shaped like a flowing body of water and composed of single timber sheets, each piece of wood has a unique curvilinear shape resembling cross-sections of a river stream. The Water-Flow Benches are both an artistic installation and casual outdoor furniture for relaxation. The smooth geometry of the benches is achieved through a combination of laser-cut technology and handmade craftsmanship. The original colouring and grain of the gold silk teak wood are sealed and exposed. Folding tables made of titanium-coated stainless steel complete the furniture and accentuate the elongated benches. The contrast of materiality between the soft, warm timber and the cool and shiny titanium mirrors the beauty of the unity of gentleness and strength. By enhancing the immanent vitality and pureness of materials through craftsmanship and design, the woodwork lets residents tune into a life with nature.

Rong Garden terrace – floating teak wood bench ››

Woodwork in tune with autumn colours ⌃

Violet Palace

Shijiazhuang, Hebei Province

Client: China Vanke Co. Ltd.
Type: exterior decoration, residential design

Size: 30,900 m²
Year: 2019

Place Shijiazhuang is the capital and largest city of northern China's Hebei province. Once a small township, the population of the metropolitan area has quadrupled in the past thirty years as a result of rapid industrialisation and infrastructure development. Shijiazhuang is situated east of the Taihang Mountains, a mountain range extending over 400 kilometres from north to south, making the city a popular holiday destination for outdoor adventure, hiking and cycling.

Approach The masterplan of Violet Palace residential development follows the traditional Chinese courtyard layout. Chinese vernacular architecture details are incorporated in all buildings. The landscape design draws on the cultural connotation of the Summer Palace as a place of repose and seeks to infuse the residential compound with the charm and grandeur of a royal garden. Moshang's furniture design at Violet Palace emphasises the correlation of space and rituals of inhabitation. Four distinct scenes were defined at the commencement of the design. Each frame refers to a human activity linked to a discrete garden setting and dates back to classic Chinese garden scenes as depicted in ancient Chinese paintings: scholars appreciating tea; listening to raindrops in the forest; watching snowflakes falling; playing music; sitting under a blossoming tree. Equally, the colour palette and motifs of the furniture design refer to traditional Chinese paintings, with red, cloudy grey and dark green as leading tones and the diamond pattern commonly found on roof tiles as the defining feature.

Design Four main scenes guide the journey through the courtyard, creating a choreographed experience in reference to the traditional life of ancient scholars.

1st scene: Clubhouse – entertaining guests in the forest. Comfort and natural textures drive the lounge furniture design. At the stone coffee table, the natural texture of the black marble is exposed and embedded into a delicate metal rim. The generous red leather cushions, the ergonomic backrest curvature, the three-way six-cup diamond engravings: all details contribute to the natural softness of the royal chairs.

2nd scene: Sunken deck – sitting by the water.
After the forest, one crosses the arched bridge and enters into the garden at the lake. Two fireplaces warm the sunken waterfront deck. "Imagine a winter evening, lighting up the fire next to the water – a beautiful purifying moment in life."

3rd scene: Lakefront – listening by the water.
A pair of single chairs stands opposite each other by the water. The dark red of the chairs contrasts with the natural colours of the bluestone, the grasses and the mist above the water. "Against the backdrop of mountains and rivers, one finds a good friend to sit next to and listen to the wind and rain – a tranquil encounter far from the noise of the city."

4th scene: Tea pavilion – enjoying the mountain scenery. Continuing the journey, one reaches the tea pavilion on the hill. The high-backed chairs and long tea table are inspired by classic Chinese furniture and further detailed by custom-made applications referencing the cornice and wall hangings in traditional Chinese architecture. "A sheltered place to share tea and enjoy the mountain scenery with friends."

Furniture collection – concept illustration ››

Material palette – stone, metal, timber, leather; royal gold, red, black ⌃

< 1st scene – Clubhouse
Entertaining guests in the forest

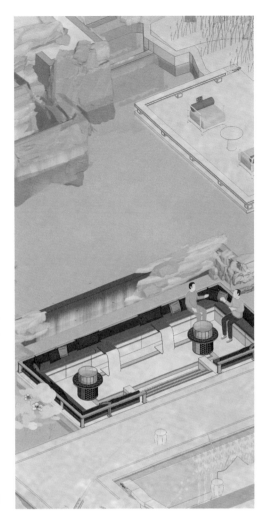

2nd scene – Sunken deck ›
Sitting by the water

< 3rd scene – Lakefront
Listening by the water

138

4th scene – Tea pavilion ›
Enjoying the mountain scenery

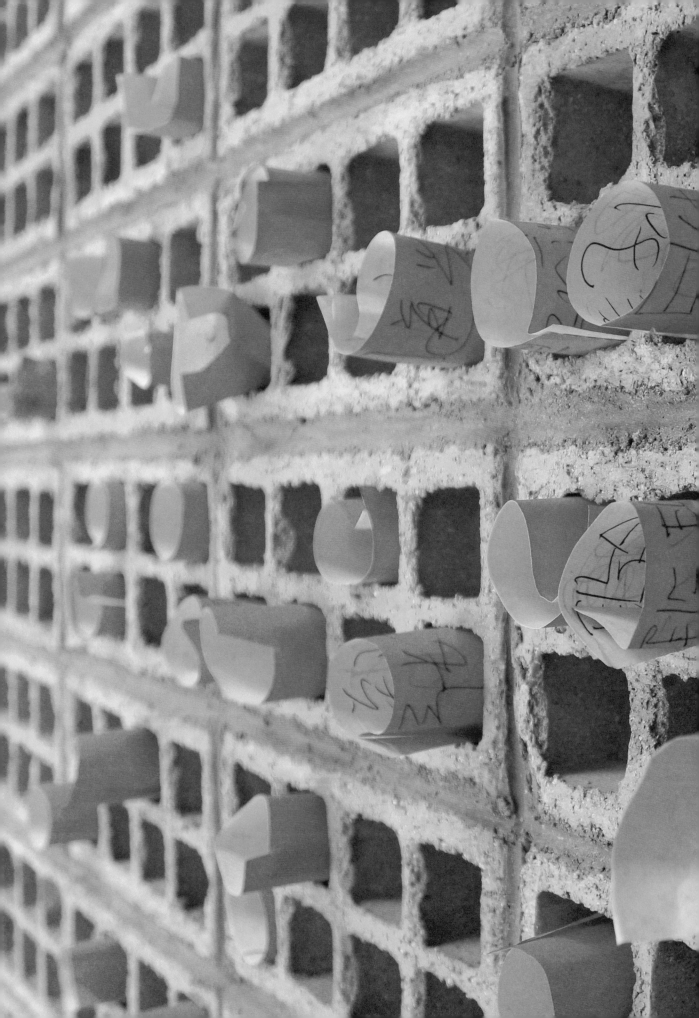

Fu Yingbin Studio

Empowerment of Rural Communities

Beijing

Fu Yingbin Studio

Beijing

Founder: Fu Yingbin
Founded: 2016
Team: 1–5
Location: Beijing
Portfolio: rural development, placemaking, community building, environmental design, landscape architecture, architecture

Fu Yingbin Studio is a transdisciplinary landscape architecture studio based in Beijing. Established in 2016 as a sub-studio under the umbrella of the China New Rural Planning and Design Institute (CNRPD), Fu Yingbin Studio is concerned with rural development through integrated architecture and landscape architecture solutions. The studio philosophy and work ethic are founded on a site-based approach. Projects are initiated, developed and constructed in intensive dialogue and participation with local rural communities. The scope of work reaches from environmental reconstruction to communal space design and the preservation of local narratives and traditions through design interventions, both architecture as well as landscape architecture based.

The work of Fu Yingbin Studio is typically embedded into a wider set of poverty alleviation measures within the townships conducted by CNRPD. Founded by Li Changping and Sun Jun, CNRPD is a widely acknowledged thought leader in rural economic development and empowerment in China. Li Changping, the President of CNRPD, initially gained nationwide attention in 2000 after penning an open letter to then-Premier of the People's Republic of China Zhu Rongji, proclaiming sharply that "farmers' lives are really miserable; rural communities are really impoverished; agriculture is really dangerous" and alerting central government to the ongoing agricultural crisis in the hinterland. Subsequently, after having served in township-level governments for seventeen years, Li Changping resigned to become a migrant worker in Guangdong and has since been advocating for equal treatment for farmers countrywide. He is the author of the Built-in Finance Theory and the rural community development model based upon this theory. The scheme promotes the establishment of rural cooperatives, which allows members of the cooperatives to collateralise their land and membership against loans and enables the capitalisation and transaction of rural resources. The model has dramatically improved farmers' income-generating capabilities and enhanced rural organisations' services for its members. Led by CNRPD, similar models and targeted poverty alleviation initiatives have been implemented nationwide. As the pioneer in the field of Built-in Finance in rural construction in China, the teams of CNRPD are dedicated to efficient, practical and economic, social and architectural solutions benefitting from cross-disciplinary resources and a clear understanding of national policies as well as industry trends.

Fu Yingbin is the Founder and Director of Fu Yingbin Studio, a landscape architecture and architecture design studio within the CNRPD network in Beijing. His studio's work is characterised by cross-disciplinary, integrated design and rural in-situ practice. Intensive dialogue and collaboration with local villagers and village representatives inform Fu Yingbin's work. He guides all projects from concept to planning and construction, achieving a modern expression in design within the specifics of the local context. Prior to founding Fu Yingbin Studio, Fu Yingbin worked at Turenscape, Beijing. He is a member of the jury of the Peking University LA Pioneer Awards. Fu Yingbin holds a Bachelor in Environmental Art and Design from Tianjin University of Science & Technology. The work of the studio has been widely published in architecture and landscape architecture magazines and academic journals in China, and was exhibited at the 2017 Shenzhen International Design Week and the 2018 Venice Architecture Biennale as part of the Building a Future Countryside group exhibition at the China Pavilion.

<< Temple of the God of Wealth – prayer wall

Fu Yingbin (l.) – team (r.) – in-situ practice >>

In conversation with Fu Yingbin about past and present agricultural reforms, rural nostalgia and architecture as an auxiliary to landscape.

Fu Yingbin Studio focuses primarily on rural development. To provide a context to your project work, could you sketch the wider social and economic conditions of China's rural hinterland – in present and past?

Fu Yingbin That is a big subject. I could write a book about this topic.

What would be your short summary, respectively?

Fu Yingbin The basic rural structure as we still see it today was formed after the founding of the People's Republic of China (PRC). Before 1949, the governance structure in rural China was distinctively different from the administrative system in the cities. Since ancient times, the country-side had relied on a clan system to rule the villages and regions. After the founding of the PRC, the Communist Party carried out a series of agrarian reforms. The clan-based model came to an end, even though overall it had been quite an effective way to govern rural issues in a self-responsible and decentralised manner. From the 1950s onwards, the villages came under the mandate of two committees: the village committee and the party representatives, which jointly oversaw the people's commune as the highest of three administrative levels in rural areas. During that period, China's rural production was closely monitored. Everyone was part of a larger collective. From food production to sales, everything was organised and distributed collectively. As we all know in the 1960s and 1970s, China suffered from famine and serious problems in the people's communes. Also, the productivity was low because it was like 'feeding all from the same big pot, where you can't tell which one is yours, all together'.

In 1982 Deng Xiaoping introduced a reform called the 'household responsibility system'. The reform was triggered by the Xiaogang incident. The village of around a hundred people in twenty households was infamous for its poverty which forced the villagers to beg after autumn harvest to support their livelihood. On the night of November 24, in 1978, 18 farmers gathered and made the bold decision to break away from the management orthodoxy of the people's commune in favour of a 'land contract system'. To show their commitment, the farmers signed the 'contract' with their fingerprints, a traditional way of sealing a promise.

It was like 'feeding all from the same big pot, where you can't tell which one is yours, all together'.

After signing, the farmers distributed the farmland and production tools. Subsequently, the farmers managed their land individually and kept the surplus of the yield beyond the state's share of the produce. Within a year, the per capita household income had increased twenty-fold, prompting other neighbouring villages to adopt the same model. This incident marked the prelude of a wide range of rural reforms in China.

I understood the reforms marked a turning point in agricultural production – for the better I assume?

Fu Yingbin Yes and no, unfortunately. The new reforms followed the Xiaogang model and the people's communes were replaced by townships following the same administrative model as the cities. The 1980s were a good time in rural China. There was a sense of prosperity, everyone was enthusiastic, and agricultural productivity rose tremendously. One needs to keep in mind that during those years everything was still in short supply. There was no sales problem, only a production problem. But from the 1990s until now, that has changed dramatically. In fact, the entire production today is in a state of oversupply, whether it is rural or urban. The problem of the countryside became reversed. While productivity increased, the sales prices achievable on the market decreased and with them household incomes.

Another factor is that through the reforms, the management capacity of the rural agencies declined. The two committees I mentioned before once had a strong steering capacity, but today every farmer is on his own without any power or influence on the market prices on a larger scale.

In retrospect, what would you consider as the root cause of the issues the countryside is facing today?

Fu Yingbin I believe the developments in the past are the root cause of China's current rural problems. Rural production today is too fragmented; the farming entities are too small, rural organisations have little power, and the whole system is too decentralised.

The small farmlands cannot support large households anymore, and young people need to leave the villages to make a living elsewhere. The countryside is over-ageing and the problem will only get worse in the near future.

I believe the developments in the past are the root cause of China's current rural problems. Rural production today is too fragmented; the farming entities are too small, rural organisations have little power, and the whole system is too decentralised. The small farmlands cannot support large households anymore, and young people need to leave the villages to make a living elsewhere. The countryside is over-ageing and the problem will only get worse in the near future.

How would you describe the current state of China's countryside?

Fu Yingbin There is no such thing as 'the' countryside in China. All regions differ substantially concerning their state of development and economic vitality. When travelling through Europe, I always found that the countryside appears to be quite equally developed. For most parts it is so beautiful, well-kept and seemingly in a state of prosperity everywhere. We have these beautiful places and regions as well. In Guizhou province, for example, some places are doing very well, and the landscape scenery is stunning. Also, the southeast coastal areas of Zhejiang, Fujian and Guangzhou provinces are quite prosperous. But again, the rural economy of these provinces doesn't rely on farming anymore, but on small workshops and local production. Similarly, the villages in Jiang Nan, the region south of the Yangtze River, benefit from good conditions. The climate there is very good, the ground fertile and the transportation network well established. The region's countryside in many ways resembles Japan's, where there is hardly any difference in the standard of life between urban and rural areas and household incomes are equally high.
But for most rural areas in China that is still not the case today. Take Guizhou province, for example, which I mentioned before. It is a mountainous province, many areas are hard to access. The landscape scenery might be pristine, but the villages are impoverished and the homesteads in decay. Another example is Shanxi province. It is a coal mining region. The climate is very dry, the soil condition poor and the environment degraded through years of mining. I saw villages there with no more than ten villagers left. It almost looked a bit spooky, like a scene from a horror movie: old people, dilapidated buildings and some stray dogs. When the remaining villagers die, the villages will most likely disappear. Of course, there were beautiful homesteads with century-old craftwork which we designers adore. But why preserve the shell, when life has vanished?

This sounds rather discouraging. Where do you see opportunities for lasting change in the countryside?

Fu Yingbin The renewal of Zhongguan village, portrayed in this book, is an encouraging example of rural development, I suppose. Let's touch the challenging parts only lightly. It is a mountainous region, with hardly any land suitable for farming. The main source of income is tobacco plantations,

I saw villages there with no more than ten villagers left. It almost looked a bit spooky, like a scene from a horror movie: old people, dilapidated buildings and some stray dogs. Of course, there were beautiful homesteads with century-old craftwork which we designers adore. But why preserve the shell, when life has vanished?

Swing above the river at Sun village – a simple and cost-efficient solution and a tribute to the children of the village ⌃

which further deteriorated the arable land. However, Zhongguan is close to Chongqing, a metropolis of 30 million people. We call Chongqing the 'furnace' of China, infamous for its unbearably hot and humid summer months. Zhongguan lies at a high altitude and Chongqingers had discovered the area as a summer retreat. Hence, villagers began refurbishing their homesteads to profit from this new and unexpected source of income. Only everything was done haphazardly. Finally, the county government stepped in and reached a loan policy agreement with the Agricultural Development Bank of China to support the renovation of villages in the area. That's when CNRPD came into play.

How do you collaborate with CNRPD?

Fu Yingbin We are separate teams, but operate under one umbrella. CNRPD takes care of the 'software', such as the organisational structure, the provisions of loans, new income-generating enterprises and the overall layout of the renewal effort. My team is in charge of the 'hardware', such as the architecture or landscape architecture works.

There is a remarkable emphasis on sustainable countryside development in China in recent years from both government as well as grassroots agencies advocating for rural tourism and local speciality production. How do you view those initiatives?

Fu Yingbin They are both valuable in their own right. They create the synergy needed for such a complex development task. My concern is how well or not these new projects and initiatives address the villagers' life and are able to support it. It is a complicated matter. There is always the risk of either overdevelopment or rural nostalgia.

Are you referring to the new hype around 'rural architectures'?

Fu Yingbin It is a controversial subject. From our point of view, which we have always insisted on, something like 'vernacular' materials do not exist. Materials are materials, not agents of 'local values'. What had been used in the past was used because it suited the conditions in the past. Farmers and builders utilised materials such as wood, bamboo or tiles as they were the easiest to obtain and control.

There is always the risk of either overdevelopment or rural nostalgia.

*From our point of view
something like 'vernacular'
materials do not exist.
For as long as a material is
suitable for this particular
environment and available
in remote areas, it is a
countryside material.*

On the contrary, I would argue, materials such as metal, prefabricated steel plates or concrete are the easiest and cheapest to obtain and control in rural areas today. In comparison, traditional or natural materials often cause problems in the process of construction and became, in fact, the 'precious' rather than the common solution. Rammed earth, for example, in the past it certainly was the cheapest building material available in the countryside. But today it simply is not. In my opinion, for as long as a material is suitable for this particular environment and available in remote areas, it is a countryside material. Therefore, we never deliberately use a particular 'local' material in order to pursue 'visual beauty' or 'authenticity'. I believe projects like the Jintai village earthquake reconstruction in Sichuan province by Rural Urban Framework (RUF) are an excellent and promising way forward. It is socially and environmentally sustainable and serves the community rather than the 'picturesque'.

Originally trained as a landscape architect, your projects encompass both architecture and landscape design. Where do you see the connection and each discipline's respective relevance in the countryside?

Fu Yingbin In the city, the disciplines are divided but the countryside is different. This division of labour does not exist. Also, the relationship with the landscape is always very direct and close. At large buildings, the landscape is often the 'auxiliary' structure, at the small buildings we do it is rather the opposite: the built form supports the landscape. In comparison, I don't think the villages need a 'designed' landscape. The task is rather to preserve the existing natural environment. Also, maintenance is a big issue. In our new protects we rather refrain from any landscape design and instead invest in the reviving of production landscapes which are beautiful and profit-generating at the same time.

To ask the first question last – why this interest in the countryside?

*I am interested in design as
'utopia' – anything else is just
'icing on the cake'.*

Fu Yingbin The work with the villagers is close to my ideal way of working. I always wanted to do projects which address social issues and where you can dig into a subject and find new and meaningful solutions. This is actually also the case with 'urban villages', the former old towns in Chinese cities. But that is another huge topic. I am interested in design as 'utopia' – anything else is just 'icing on the cake'. Who needs it?

Zhongguan Village Renewal

Zheng'an County, Guizhou Province

Client: Zheng'an County People's Government
Type: participatory design, public space

Size: varies
Year: 2016

Place Zhongguan village is a small township in Zheng'an county, in the north of Guizhou province. While rich in natural, cultural and environmental resources, the landlocked mountainous province in the west of China has not substantially benefitted from China's opening and economic reform policies in the past four decades. The province has the third-lowest GDP per capita in China, only ahead of Gansu province and neighbouring Yunnan. In contrast, Guizhou province has one of the fastest-growing economies in China, with central government developing the urban area of Guizhou city into a national Big Data hub. Life in the countryside, however, remains poor and economically underdeveloped, with villagers left with few alternatives other than traditional subsistence farming to support their livelihoods and young people leaving their hometowns to work in the prosperous cities.

Approach Communication and respect are key to Fu Yingbin Studio's practice in the countryside. "I believe the renewal of the countryside should put people first. The task is not just simply to help paint or repair or plant but to directly engage with the people. We may believe villagers to be conservative, whereas they are actually willing to accept new things. If there are conflicts, reasonable explanations will convince them. Most conflicts are about manners and customs. Respect is the guarantor of a project's smooth development. We usually discuss the details with the village cadres and elders in order to avoid offending their customs. Communicating ahead of acting is important. Only by respecting the villagers and their way of life will innovative changes be accepted. Compared to the people, the design is not that important. Our projects are not pure design items but systemic solutions. We are not only concerned with spatial design but also target rural financial problems. The ultimate goal is that the villages can economically function again and further develop

independently by themselves," outlines Fu Yingbin the bottom-up approach of his studio work in the countryside.

Design Over the course of eight months, during which the team worked in Zhongguan village, Fu Yingbin Studio identified and realised six projects in the township in close collaboration with the village committee: the Pedestrian Bridge, the Furnace of Words, the Long March Memorial, the Children's Playground and Recycling Centre, the Tobacco Curing Barn Homestay and the Village Library. All design work was done on site and drawing-free. Materials were sourced locally and directly assembled on-site. Construction methods were tailored to local conditions and the manpower available. All structures were built in a robust and durable way, with low maintenance required in the future.

1. Pedestrian Bridge
2. Furnace of Words
3. Long March Memorial
4. Community Playground and Recycling Centre
5. Tobacco Curing Barn Homestay
6. Village Library

0   10 m   50 m   100 m

"We are not building one bridge, but two. One is the bridge of substance, the other is between people and the second one is more important," summarises Fu Yingbin the design team's intentions for the pedestrian bridge in Zhongguan village.

Local people's lives are closely tied to the river, which divides the small village into two parts. Power lines dangle across the river. With water levels rising during rainy season, the electricity lines are frequently submerged and crossing the river on foot without a bridge becomes impossible. Thus, a pedestrian bridge was urgently needed. Construction methods and materials had to be simple and sourced locally, taking into consideration that no long-distance transport costs for construction materials could have been afforded and all manpower and construction work had to be carried out by the villagers themselves. The lack of workforce became an additional concern. As in most rural areas, the parent

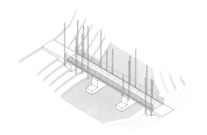

generation is missing in the village. Young people have left their impoverished hometowns for work in the thriving cities along the coast to support the grandparents and children who remain in the village. There has been an unforeseen advantage, however. With migrant workers frequently labouring in construction, they brought with them respectable technical skills when returning to the village during their annual Spring Festival break.

Gabion walls were chosen as construction material for the base of the bridge. Commonly applied in river and slope restoration, the galvanised steel wire cages are easy to construct and could be filled with local stones from the mountains. In order to ensure sufficient gravity, the piers were built in hull form, measuring one by four metres on a concrete foundation. Finally, three-span steel girders were carried to the site and welded into a single structure. ››

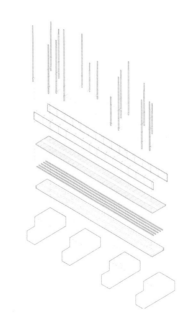

<< Substructure – existing pedestrian crossing, collective construction effort, gabion piers

^ Bridge cladding – low cost, prefabricated, galvanised steel panels and metal mesh

^ Soft fitting – bamboo railing and light poles, natural materials blending into the landscape

Zhongguan Village **Village Footbridge**

After completion of the structural parts of the bridge, the team of designers and local villagers focused on the final cladding and fitting of the bridge. Also here, simplicity, cost efficiency and local availability were prioritised in the selection of fixtures. Perforated steel planks, widely used for scaffolding, are utilised as deck material for the pedestrian passage. The galvanised steel boards offer resistance against friction, pressure and corrosion and met the criteria of a light and trans-parent appearance of the bridge design. In addition, a 60-centimetre-wide steel band runs across the bridge to accommodate easy passage. To soften the industrial look of the bridge, the designers added local bamboo canes as a design feature of the handrails and the light poles. The natural cavity of the bamboo canes is utilised as a cable duct for the lighting wires and cut in half at the top to serve as a reflection screen for the recessed lighting. After nightfall, the soft light of the poles adds

"We are not building one bridge, but two. One is the bridge of substance, the other is between people and the second one is more important."

‹ A safe and comfortable passage in all seasons and a place to socialise and play

Evening impression – a symbol of connectivity and a subtle landmark for the village ››

154

poetry to the village. Day and night, the bamboo poles and wild reeds along the river appear to unite the bridge and nature into a single organic whole.

The most auspicious date and time to install the structural frame was calculated by the alderman of the village. After the opening ceremony, the sound of firecrackers echoed through the valley. Today, children run across the bridge with excitement, young couples lean on the railing and elderly villagers appreciate the safety and convenience of the new connection. The bridge has created a new village commodity for all. As Fu Yingbin points out: "The bridge not only solved a traffic problem but became a new community site. Irrespective of the width or the danger of the river, we believe that the action jointly taken in building the bridge was even more significant than the result. It is the connection between people of both banks and the new ties established that will last forever in the long river of time."

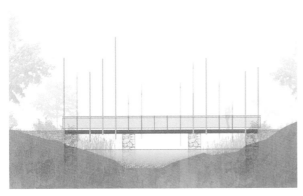

Guizhou province still retains an old Chinese custom: 'Respecting the Words on Paper'. In ancient times, written letters were sacred symbols of culture, and people worshipped handwritten scripts on paper. Thus, paper could not be thrown away at random. Every family had a paper-collecting basket hanging at a blessed place. After collection, the words were burned and the ashes taken to rivers and lakes, a folk custom called 'sending the word ash'.

The custom is still alive in Zhongguan village, yet there was no ceremonial space to burn the paper. A platform at the riverbank next to the old village temple was the location of choice by the villagers to revive the folk tradition. The timeworn temple built from clifftop rocks was restored and the river embankment solidified and covered with a steel plate deck. In ancient times, the word-burning furnaces in the region were usually built in the form of a masonry tower and its hollow inside

used for the firing process. However, as a new auxiliary facility to the village temple, the shape and volume of the furnace needed to be carefully reconsidered, in order to avoid any notion of competing in appearance with the village temple. Therefore, the shape of the Furnace of Words was simplified and reduced to a minimalist steel column. The slender column now rests next to the stone temple, creating a dialogue of shapes and materials, each in respect of its time of origin.

Traditional verses of worship were punched through the steel plates on opposite sides of the column. Word-burning ceremonies are usually carried out in the evening. At night, a scene of mystery is reborn in the village: the fire of the burning paper suffuses the furnace with light, and smoke slowly fades through the openings of the stencilled-out verses. The pouring of the ashes into the river below by the village chief concludes the revived ritual and the words can float again as in the olden times.

‹‹ 'Respecting the Words on Paper' – household paper collection basket

‹‹ Village temple in original state and after restoration ›

‹‹ Word-burning ceremony – fire illuminating inscriptions
Restored village temple and word-burning stele ⌄

Zhongguan Village **Long March Memorial and Tomb**

In the course of the village renovation, the designers learned of the grave of an unknown soldier and the only man in the village who knew about it: an eighty-year-old villager. During the Long March, the Battle of Loushanguan (1935) took place 12 kilometres southwest of the village. After the ambush, an ill young soldier was left behind in the village. The old man's father took care of the boy and later buried his remains on the family land. The young son continued to tend the grave ever since. Now elderly himself, the burial site had become overgrown and had almost disappeared.

The villagers opted to honour this village chronicle with a remembrance site. In respect to its humble origins, the new memorial is designed as a commemorative landscape integrated into the forested hills, a modest gesture and quiet place for contemplation. A 2.5-kilometre-long memorial route leads to the site. The small path is intentionally uneven, symbolising the Chinese Red Army's

‹ Overgrown burial site of the abandoned soldier of the Battle of Loushanguan (1935)

The caretakers of the grave for eighty years, on their first visit to the new memorial site ⌄

158

strenuous 25,000-li-long march. Eighteen steel panels accompany the route. They record important events along the march, ranked chronologically. The memorial pavilion forms the spatial climax of the sequence. The airy corten steel structure cantilevers out over the hillside. It not only marks the entrance to the memorial but also serves as a resting place to gaze back at the village and to contemplate present and past. From afar, only the pavilion can be seen; all other sections of the remem-

brance route are hidden in the surrounding hills. The corten steel structures and stonewalls built from local rock blend into the colours and materiality of the natural environment and will ever more so while weathering. When approaching the memorial, a limestone wall retains the sloping ground, slowly rising from the soil and gradually returning to it. For the designers, it symbolises "a small wave in the entire river of history – a young life that had forever struggled and then disappeared." ››

Landscape pavilion – a landmark of the hidden memorial from afar and an outlook over the village today ⌃

Fu Yingbin Studio Zhongguan Village Renewal, Zheng'an County

Zhongguan Village **Long March Memorial and Tomb**

Inside the memorial grounds, weathered corten steel boards arise from the earth and delineate the path. Engravings on each board pay tribute to the numerous unnamed soldiers who gave their lives along the march. From there, the narrow passage bends one last time and guides the visitors to the furthest destination of the path: the plaque and grave of Hou Zhongmao.

As Fu Yingbin describes the design team's intention:

"After the completion of the Long March Memorial and Tomb, the old man, who had seen the Chinese Red Army on the march at a young age and safeguarded the grave for almost eighty years, deliberately came to visit the memorial. He cried in front of the grave. Casual visitors also admit this is a different martyrs' cemetery experience. In our design, we tried to avoid the usual grand narrative and pathos of this kind of place and aimed instead to represent the traces of the life of an ordinary

A quiet place of contemplation – immersed in the forest, hidden and secluded ˄

Corten steel panels along the memorial path – chronologically recording the main events of the Long March ››

‹ Weathered steel boards rising from the ground – in remembrance of the unknown soldiers of the Long March

soldier from the perspective of all human beings. There are no tall monuments in this space, no axial symmetry, no ceremoniousness. On the contrary, the space is full of warmth and quiet remembrance. In the past, the majority of commemorative landscape designs were dedicated to gods, emperors, war heroes or other outstanding figures. But even ordinary people often cast a divine shadow. In this project, we honour the ordinary Chinese Red Army soldiers. No heroic deeds, no title, but only a man of mere flesh and blood, taking on the brilliance of divinity. Hou Zhongmao's quiet existence and death actually represent the ordinary people who once lived in this village, too: the ones as silent and unrecognised as he was in his tribute to the future of the country. This is exactly what we as designers want to express about the humanism of war: a memorial to the respect for life and the recognition of the value of each individual's existence and lasting significance."

Zhongguan Village **Community Playground and Recycling Centre**

When the design team first arrived in Zhongguan, the children of the village caught their attention. As in most rural areas the parents work in the cities, their financial resources barely allowing them to safeguard the upbringing of their children, let alone to influence how they are raised. Similarly, most rural renewal efforts are centred around poverty alleviation policies and economic development. None of this ever directly benefits children. Fu Yingbin's team decided to give to the young generation by creating a simple and joyful playground in the centre of the village. The ongoing village reconstruction had left piles of mechanical and building waste on the site, deemed unusable for future construction. However, this way of thinking accounts for the logic and regulations applied in cities; the logic of the countryside is different: stitching, patching, repairing and reinventing are the modus operandi of life here. The design for the playground appreciates these uncer-

Designing with blanks: no drawing nor plan, but creativity and fun – villagers building their own playground from basic building materials and reused construction waste

‹ Abandoned pipes turned into whispering devices and discovery tunnels

Children imprinting their palm- and footprints on the wet cement ›

Villagers erecting walls and small structures and inking well-wishes – a collective effort filling the blanks of the design with life ⌄

tainties. No plan was drawn, and a lot of blanks were left in the design at the start of the construction. The design team prepared pigments and cement, and the villagers spontaneously filled in the blanks. Children imprinted leaves of plants or their own palm- and footprints in the wet cement. The village alderman inked a Taoist blessing for peace and health on a broken column. Leftover sewage pipes were turned into discovery tunnels, metal tubes into whispering devices. Furthermore, the site was cleared of debris and materials sorted for reuse.

"A tree shakes another tree, a cloud pushes another cloud, and a soul awakens another soul. This creates freedom and awakens life." With this proverb, Fu Yingbin illustrates the rationale behind his team's work and their emphasis on bottom-up and lasting transformation. "We hope that our work will bring a little bit of positive change to the villages and all change starts with the care for the next generation."

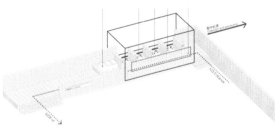

Recycling and Environmental Learning Centre – clearing the site of construction debris and sorting of material in recycling compartments, for in-situ reuse and distribution >

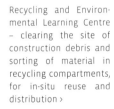

Rural Acupuncture

Sun Village, Huoshan County, Anhui Province

Client: Sun Township People's Government
Type: participatory design, public space

Size: varies
Year: 2018

Place Sun township is located in the heart of the scenic area of the Dabie Mountains in Huoshan county, Anhui province. The Dabie Mountains are a major mountain range in central China; running northwest-to-southeast, they form the main watershed between the Huai and Yangtze rivers. The mountains also mark the boundary between Hubei province and its neighbours of Henan to the north and Anhui to the east. The range is heavily forested, with about 85 per cent coverage, and yields bamboo as well as oak, particularly cork oak, making it China's chief cork-producing area. Still, the region's median household income is below China's rural average, and subsistence agriculture, predominantly rice and tea plantations, are the primary source of income.

Approach Unlike the comprehensive renovation in Zhongguan village, Fu Yingbin Studio's work in Sun village is guided by the principle of 'rural acupuncture'. The approach gives preference to design interventions and incentives for change in perception, with each 'acupuncture node' stimulating long-term sustainable 'healing' rather than providing only impromptu short-term solutions. Three village renewal projects punctuate the township today, each addressing the flaws of China's ongoing urbanisation of the countryside. Conjointly, they establish showcase examples for the preservation of local customs and vernacular landscape typologies, and for site-sensitive adaptations of standardised infrastructure works.

Design Also, in Sun village no brief was initially provided when Fu Yingbin Studio's team first arrived. Instead, the projects and design briefs evolved step by step, based on the findings made during the work in progress and discussions with the villagers. In total, three projects were identified, each pointing at a crucial issue in recent countryside development:
First, ecological problems caused by the urbanisation of the hinterland, such as the extensive hardening of terrains. Heavily engineered road infrastructure works and the revetment of riverbeds are changing the pace and habits of rural life. The low-budget retrofitting of the village road and bridge in Sun village presents an alternative solution within the given structural constraints.

Second, the preservation of vernacular landscapes which had been sustained by local subsistence farming for decades and had started to decline and wane. The rice terraces and tea plantations of Sun township, once the omnipresent production landscape in the region and intrinsically linked to the village life, are in retreat. The new Youth Academy in a converted farmhouse overlooking a basin of fields evokes a different view of the past and revives the tradition of 'Farming and Reading' in a contemporary manner.

Third, the respect of folk customs and the preservation of religious sites, which tend to disappear unnoticed during the process of modernisation. The new Temple of the God of Wealth pays tribute to local customs and reinvigorates a tiny and almost forgotten sacred site as a modern place of worship.

Sun village – project locations ››

Temple of the God of Wealth – before restoration ⌃

1. Harvesting Pavilion
2. Rice Terraces
3. Youth Academy
4. Temple of the God of Wealth
5. Road Bridge Renovation

0 2 m   10 m   50 m

Sun Village **Rice Field Restoration and Youth Academy**

'Farming and Reading' is a life creed Chinese people have believed in since ancient times. The Youth Academy above the rice terraces is designed in line with this traditional Chinese cultural theme. Originally the rural home of an elderly couple, the township government commissioned Fu Yingbin Studio to convert the old farmhouse into a community facility for the residents and a display area for local tea culture. The site is located at the centre of the market town, yet still feels tranquil and natural. Forests surround the small basin of rice terraces, bisected by a narrow creek. The old homestead towers above the terrain overlooking the valley of fields. Lush and full of ambience now, the site lacked character and showed a rather bland appearance before renovation. The rice fields were sparsely maintained. The creek line was devoid of planting. With rice paddies being the landscape typology most common in the province, the original intent of the village council had been to replace

< Farming and *Reading*

Youth Academy – converted farmstead and new annexe
Old barn reading room
Restored creek line and path

the 'ordinary' production landscape with a decorative 'special' one: a flower garden. Through several rounds of meetings Fu Yingbin Studio convinced the township leaders to value the vernacular, and the rice terraces were restored. Today, the renewed rice fields, together with tea plantations and vegetable gardens, define the landscape character of the site. Cultivated by their original owners, the production landscapes became a place for casual strolls and learning. They actively link the programme of both the landscape and the buildings. The Harvesting Pavilion situated across the basin from the Youth Academy echoes the college buildings and furthermore strengthens the interlacing of architecture and farming.

Since the completion of the Youth Academy, the children of the town come to the library after school every afternoon to do their homework and play, just as their ancestors pursued 'Farming and Reading' for millennia.

Farming and Reading ›

Rice Terraces and Harvesting Pavilion
Preservation of vernacular production
landscapes and local traditions

Sun Village **Village Road and Bridge Upgrade**

After the completion of the Youth Academy, the local government approached Fu Yingbin Studio to advise on the improvement of the village bridge at the entrance of the site. The recently built road bridge had been the result of a river reconstruction. In order to gain more developable land, the rice fields on both sides of the river had been cleared and the natural riverbed channelled between revetment walls. Equally, the bridge design itself had been derived from a generic engineering solution, irrespective of local specifics. In order to adapt the bridge design to its local context and to provide additional pedestrian space on the bridge, the designers extended the bridge at either side by a cantilevered platform and replaced the original concrete balustrades with light and transparent bamboo railings. Raised planters with integrated timber seating were added along the road, greening the bridge and shielding the pedestrian walkways from traffic. Today, the bridge is a

‹ Green retrofitting and extension of pedestrian space

‹ A place to socialise and play

A place to rest and observe the river flow ⌄

fine place to unwind and observe the river stream passing underneath the grate of the bridge extension.

A second concern was the space below the bridge. Huge rocks and boulders shape the riverbed. Eroded rock formations create natural platforms funnelling river water. Even after the engineering of the embankments, people still came here to sit by the water, wash their clothes or enjoy the cooling breeze, while children played on the rocks shaded by the bridge. To improve this space, within a limited budget and in a user-friendly, yet high-water-resilient manner, the designers opted for three simple swings: one placed above the water stream and two above the rock plateaus. To reach the swing above the water, one has to walk through shallow water while swinging, one's feet still gently skim the water. The common play equipment placed in an uncommon fashion brought new fun to the river and turned the site into an active place again.

Activating the space below the bridge ›

A simple low-budget solution – creating surprise and fun ›
Common play equipment placed in an uncommon context

Sun Village **Temple of the God of Wealth**

It all began with a parking area. To support the tourism industry in Huoshan county, Fu Yingbin Studio was commissioned to design a square and car park at the foothills of the Dabie Mountains. Once the field engineering was concluded, only a small temple had not yet been torn down. The small shrine was dedicated to the God of Wealth, a common guardian god in the region, worshipped at numerous sites. As such, the decision to remove the shrine had caused little attention at first glance. After further investigation, the unpretentious temple quickly revealed itself as a sacred site for two hundred years which had been torn down and rebuilt many times. While small in size, the temple had been the spiritual centre for the local villagers for centuries and the decision was made to rebuild the shrine nearby, to permit locals to continue worshipping and to provide an additional point of interest for tourists visiting the Dabie Mountains.

‹ Temple of the God of Wealth – a continuum of space connecting the sacred realm with the landscape

Uniting modern materiality with traditional crafts – hand-woven bamboo liners creating a natural concrete surface pattern ⌄

As often in the work of Fu Yingbin Studio, the renewal of the temple became a self-initiated design task beyond the primary project brief. The designers hope that the reconstruction of this tiny, decrepit facility will contribute to the acknowledgement of ordinary folk beliefs and create a new and dignified place for rural religious rites.

The new temple was erected in a ravine in close proximity to its previous location. The renewed sanctuary is backed by mountains from three sides, as traditionally intended. Its design nonetheless contrasts with tradition. Instead of an enclosed offering space, the designer opted for an open pavilion. With the exception of the required prayer wall at the back, all other walling was omitted in favour of a continuum of space between the sacred realm and the landscape. The roof appears to float above the space, extending generously beyond the inner core and granting shelter from the rain. ››

Prayer wall – paper blessings gradually filling the hollow masonry blocks ⌃

Sun Village **Temple of the God of Wealth**

Although traditional materials can best meet the required values and aesthetics, high cost and the shortage of skilled workers make them not the best of choices. Therefore, the designers chose the most controllable and easily available material to construct the overall frame of the pavilion: in-situ concrete. Local craftsmen were invited to weave handmade bamboo mats as liners for the construction moulds. All exposed concrete surfaces of the temple now show a texture of bamboo weave, juxtaposing modern neutral materiality with the warmth of traditional crafts. The prayer wall and balustrades of the temple are built from hollow bricks. Low-cost filling blocks were used, not originally intended for visible masonry. With a simple shift in the orientation of the blocks, a perforated brick wall was created; a unique design feature built from the most ordinary of materials. The natural texture of the unalloyed bricks adds extra colour to the space. The perforated walls

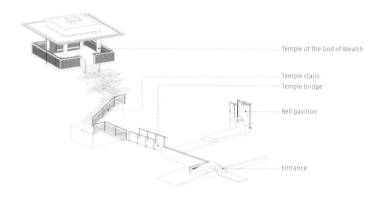

Temple of the God of Wealth
Temple stairs
Temple bridge
Bell pavilion
Entrance

New temple location and ritual passage ∧

< Roof water collection chain

Bell pavilion >

partially conceal and reveal the surrounding scenery, blurring the boundary of the space, especially at night when subtle rays of light illuminate the temple space. The square-shaped opening of the roof additionally enhances the religious atmosphere.

While the new setting of the temple surrounded by forests and hills was a flawless choice with regard to religious traditions, it raised concerns about fire safety. Not only would temple goers burn incense during daily blessings, but would furthermore light firecrackers, pine branches and paper money on special occasions. The hollow brick wall at the rear of the pavilion offered a much-appreciated solution: worshippers now roll up their paper blessing wishes and slot them into the prayer wall, instead of burning paper. Over the course of the months passing, the brick holes gradually filled with red paper sleeves; the passage of time ever more strongly uniting the built form and the believers.

WISTO

Vitality of Space

Chongqing
Shanghai
Zhengzhou

WISTO
Chongqing, Shanghai, Zhengzhou

Founder: Gao Jinghua, Li Hui
Founded: 2005
Team: 150–200
Location: Chongqing, Shanghai, Zhengzhou
Portfolio: public parks and plazas, mixed-use commercial and residential design, tourism design and planning, environmental design and urban farming

WISTO was established in 2005 by Li Hui and Gao Jinghua. Over the past fifteen years, WISTO has grown from a small landscape architecture practice in Chongqing to a network of studios with over 200 members of staff and office branches in Shanghai and Zhengzhou. The studios' project portfolio ranges from mixed-use commercial to residential design, public parks and plazas, and tourism planning and resort design. With over three hundred built projects in more than thirty cities throughout China, WISTO is one of the leading landscape architecture firms in China today.

While most of the renowned design practices are located at the main creative hubs in the metropolises along the coastline, namely Beijing, Shanghai, Guangzhou and Shenzhen, WISTO stands out with its origin and head office in Chongqing in western China. Surrounded by the mountainous green hinterland of China, WISTO's work is strongly influenced by the land and its vernacular texture. Their designs derive from the notion that each land has a 'grammatical structure' akin to a poem's. Thus, WISTO perceives their responsibility as landscape architects as learning to read and interpret this core 'grammar' of culture and tradition, without preconceptions and superimposition of design aspirations. Only then can natural elements grow in their vitality and the unique spirit of the land be passed on to the next generation through artistic conceptualisation: "From the texture of the earth to the structure of the human mind, from spring flowers in the fields to autumn leaves in the city, from the heart of the cities to the mountain plains and river valleys: it is the vitality of space throughout the years and the emotions of life, as it continues, that interests us. Only by being open to all possibilities in life can new possibilities be created."

In conversation with Gao Jinghua and Li Hui about respect for the land, urban farming as a lifestyle credo and the relationship between Chinese philosophy and landscape design.

In Chinese your studio is called Wei Tu. What does the name imply?

Gao Jinghua It is a combination of 'latitude' (Wei) and 'image' (Tu). In geography, the sky defines the zenith and the ground is represented by

Gao Jinghua is the President of WISTO and heads the operational management and business development across all studio locations. Gao Jinghua is a pioneer in urban farming and the creator of the organic farming project at the Chongqing office. In addition, she proactively supports environmental education and knowledge-sharing through publications, charities and network groups. Gao Jinghua is a Registered Urban Planner (PRC) and holds a Bachelor of Marketing from the Technology and Business University in Chongqing.

Li Hui is the Design President of WISTO. Li Hui's creations are rooted in the interrelationship of people, the scenery and the land. Designing for humanity, healing people and nature and conveying goodwill through every aspect of the design is core to WISTO's work. Li Hui is a Registered Urban Planner (PRC) and Class 1 Registered Landscape Architect (PRC). She holds a Master of Urban Planning from the School of Architecture and Urban Planning at Chongqing University and is currently enrolled in a PhD programme at the School of Architecture and Urban Planning at Chongqing University.

the grid of latitudes and longitudes. The same layering is used in weaving. Here, Wei represents the weft or 'grid' of the basic horizontal threads which are interlaced through the warp – jointly creating a beautiful canvas with each stitch and thread of the warp and weft. Our landscape design is inspired by this processual attitude of textile workers and aims to weave beautiful blueprints and images of life on every inch of the land.

Could you elaborate on this notion of landscape architecture as a process of 'weaving' upon the land?

Gao Jinghua It is important for us to respect the land and to approach any change of the land in our designs with a light touch, like a weave. For millennia, China was an agrarian society, and Chinese people have a strong attachment to the land. The ideal life, as described by ancient scholars, has always been the pastoral life. It is the ideal state of life we all yearn for. China's industrialisation and urbanisation happened particularly late – over a hundred years later than in the West. China's opening and reform took place a mere forty years ago. Many Chinese citizens today, in fact, grew up in the countryside and if not, then their parents likely did. Hence, we know that the land nourishes us. It is inherent in our traditional culture, from literature to painting and decorative objects, where we can still sense the beautiful scenes that originate from the land, whether from nature or from rural life.

For example, the famous phrase 'while picking chrysanthemums beneath the eastern fence, my gaze rests leisurely upon the southern mountain' – from the classics of Tao Hua Yuan (The Peach Blossom Spring) by Tao Yuanming, a poet during the Eastern Jin dynasty (266–420 CE) – we all know this fable of the ideal utopian place to live. There would be 'chickens clucking and dogs barking', there would be mulberries, crops and vegetable fields, which is equivalent to a picture of having ample clothing and food.

There is a striking contrast between the ancient lyrics and the reality of China's countryside today. How do you confront the issue of land and nature preservation in your work?

Gao Jinghua Different people do different things. Some people care for society and the future of the planet, while others merely pursue their own personal interests. I think it is a human commonality. To us, it is vital

For millennia, China was an agrarian society, and Chinese people have a strong attachment to the land. We know that the land nourishes us. It is inherent in our traditional culture, from literature to painting and decorative objects, where we can still sense the beautiful scenes that originate from the land, whether from nature or from rural life.

to respect the land. That doesn't imply neglecting progress and change, but those should happen while maintaining the original texture of the land and without degrading its soil and natural processes. We strongly uphold this principle in our designs, not only in the countryside but also in our work in the cities.

Li Hui As landscape architects, it is our responsibility as a profession to be concerned about the land and the protection of the environment. We have been practising for nearly twenty years and we always thought: What can landscape architecture provide to the world? And our answer is: Through the design of landscapes, we can heal the land and the people who live on the land. We always approach our designs from these two 'dimensions', the needs of people and the needs of nature, and the hope of being able to relink and repair the relationship between both.

For example, when we worked on a project in a residential community which mainly served the elderly, we volunteered in a nursing home to better understand the living environment and concerns of the elderly. What scale would best suit them? What windshield? What lighting conditions? Where to place the crutches, the ubiquitous thermos? The elderly in China often take care of the grandchildren, so how can we integrate the needs of both age groups in a public space design? How do older people feel about using a pool? What are their safety concerns? It is the same with the land. Each site's ecology is different, the water resources, the soil conditions, the microclimate, the selection of native plants. Hence the measurements for site restoration differ.

WISTO's projects often integrate agriculture and sustainable planning. The outdoor areas of your Chongqing studio are designated for urban farming. What drives this holistic approach to work and life?

Gao Jinghua Farming and respect for nature defines our work but also the life beyond. Li Hui and I both tend vegetable gardens at our homes and also at our studio space we practise urban farming. It is based on a lifestyle concept called Half-farming and Half-X, which originally stems from Japan. The idea behind is to engage partially in farming and in a professional life. No matter what occupation one has, next to it one should spend time farming to understand the cycle of life. There are many different industries and services where people work, but there is

We always approach our designs from these two 'dimensions', the needs of people and the needs of nature, and the hope of being able to relink and repair the relationship between both.

only one that human life depends upon – agriculture. When you work in the fields with your own hands, you gain more respect for food and food production. You learn about the seasons and natural processes, from water resources to planting cycles. The better one understands, the more one cherishes food, nature and the work of farmers. I think Half-farming is very meaningful in this respect. It is a way of life. But it also yields a lot of happiness. It is great to observe members of staff at our studio discussing the planting schedules for the year, joining forces in preparing the fields and picking the harvest together. Sure, in the group we also have Wugu Bu Fen, as we call people who know little about farming and literally 'cannot distinguish five grains'. Times are changing and young people growing up in the city do not learn about vegetables and fruits anymore. In this respect, our studio garden also has an educational role.

Li Hui We attach great importance to nature education and manual skills. Every Sunday we offer Waldorf classes to the children of the staff. Sometimes the teacher takes them to the gardens to pick vegetables and cook together. That's very sweet. They also use the plants in the garden as dyes for small paper tissue flowers.

Gao Jinghua There is another lesson, too. During the cultivation of the fields, one can observe the full organic cycle of plants, from seeding to growth, ripeness, harvest and decay. Composting is an important part of urban farming. There is nothing 'useless' in nature. The concept of 'waste' is a human invention. In fact, everything is part of an ever-ongoing cycle of nature, which is also reflected in Chinese philosophy.

In which respect is your work influenced by Chinese philosophy?

Li Hui Chinese philosophy and the arts, also garden art, are very closely intertwined. Confucianism and Daoism form the core of Chinese philosophy. It is a deep-rooted shared cultural understanding and heritage. No matter which dynasty, no matter from which nation the ruling class originated, they all accepted and observed this cultural codex and inheritance. A good example to illustrate this handing down of culture through the centuries is the preservation of buildings of cultural significance. Chinese traditional architectures are wooden structures. Unlike Western stone buildings, they aren't permanent. Hence, cultural

It is based on a lifestyle concept called Half-farming and Half-X. The idea behind is to engage partially in farming and in a professional life. No matter what occupation one has, next to it one should spend time farming to understand the cycle of life. There are many different industries and services, where people work, but there is only one that human life depends upon – agriculture.

Landscape restoration – Tibetan gesang flower meadows at the Village of Return ⌃

buildings in China were destroyed and rebuilt, destroyed and rebuilt many times, but their forms and structural layout never changed. Year by year, century by century, dynasty to dynasty the replacement of physical structures never destroyed the system as such, which was passed down from generation to generation. Similarly, as time progressed the codex of the rules of life, the ethic of relationships and the core aesthetics have never changed. This attitude also originates from China's farming culture, the connection with the land and the stability of family structures.

Among traditional Chinese arts, people most appreciate Shan Shui, traditional mountain-water ink paintings. Shan Shui techniques emphasise abstraction. Ink paintings are neither realistic nor as rigorous or rational as Western art, which tends to interpret the world. In contrast, ancient Chinese poets and painters cherished higher spiritual enjoyment beyond the material world. The thickness of the ink and the haziness of Shan Shui paintings express this abstract and ideal perception of life. It has been said that from the Wei dynasty (220–266 CE) to the Jin dynasty (266–420 CE) and the Southern and Northern dynasties (386–589 CE), the literati masters as the Seven Sages of the Bamboo Groves and Tao Yuan-ming (365–427 CE) introduced ideal landscapes where everyone enjoys a utopian spiritual life. Later, during the Tang (618–907) and Song dynasties (960–1279), masters such as Wang Wei (699–759) enhanced the notion of those ideals in people's minds in poems and paintings like his renowned Twenty Scenes of Wangchuan Ji. Finally, the famous gardens of the Ming (1368–1644) and Qing dynasties (1644–1912), such as the Humble Administrator's Garden (1509) and the Lingering Garden (1593) in Suzhou expressed the ideal habitat for body and mind in a physical space.

In summary, traditional Chinese paintings and gardens created a scene that originated from nature but was higher than nature. They depict an elegant lifestyle which at the same time is highly cultivated and entrenched in spiritual beliefs. A lifestyle, furthermore, that the literati always shared not only with scholars but also with the illiterate. This unity of humanity and nature in nature is the ideal that was emphasised and inherited through generations and still resonates with Chinese people today.

Longfor Island received widespread praise for its modern interpretation of traditional garden art. Could you explain the composition of space and which particular scenes or elements you applied?

Shan Shui techniques emphasise abstraction. Ink paintings are neither realistic nor as rigorous or rational as Western art, which tends to interpret the world. In contrast, ancient Chinese poets and painters cherished higher spiritual enjoyment beyond the material world. The thickness of the ink and the haziness of Shan Shui paintings express this abstract and ideal perception of life.

Traditional Chinese paintings and gardens created a scene that originated from nature but was higher than nature.

Li Hui Longfor Island is based upon four modes of spatial compositions: Sishui Guitang, Bu Yi Jing Yi, Gao Shan Liu Shui and bamboo curtains. Sishui Guitang means 'four waters return to the courtyard' and describes the traditional Chinese courtyard, where all eaves faced inward collecting the rainwater of the roofs from all four cardinal directions in a central basin in the yard. The water was an essential commodity for all residents and was used for both fire protection and production. The curved floating roof at Longfor Island is designed as a reminiscence of the Sishui Guitang courtyard family house. Another principle we applied is Bu Yi Jing Yi, 'one step one scene'. Chinese gardens are composed as a sequence of two-dimensional key scenes, with each scene depicting a perfect image of nature and obtaining a different experience for the observer. Another aspect is the expression of nature as in Gao Shan Liu Shui, 'high mountains flowing water'. The elevation difference on site provided the opportunity to create a cascading water feature, recalling the sound of a mountain spring and river streams. The fourth aspect, which supports the principle of Bu Yi Jing Yi, is the screening and framing of scenes through bamboo curtains. In our design, we used the thin steel columns of the Sishui Guitang roof to simulate a bamboo curtain. The spacing of columns varies to create screening and opening effects. Going from scene to scene, they shield or open view lines and manipulate the light conditions from dim to bright to orchestrate the views and pauses along the walk.

WISTO's courtyard design differentiates itself from the currently omnipresent neoclassical style. What is your view on such trends?

They both express a view which is non-anthropocentric and regards life as deeply entrenched in nature.

Li Hui Trends don't matter much. Reviving the essence of Chinese garden art and philosophy is key. Let me close with two last Chinese phrases from Daoist and Confucian philosophy respectively: Dao Fa Ziran, meaning the Dao follows the law of nature, and Tian Ren He Yi, the unity of heaven and man. They both express a view which is non-anthropocentric and regards life as deeply entrenched in nature. In other words, material life can be simple, but the mind should transcend it. Throughout the past decades, we saw many design trends come and go, often imported ones and always succeeding each other quickly. It might be time to pause and reconsider. There is a sense of tranquillity and purity in both traditional arts and nature that resonates with us and that also refers to the beginning of our conversation, the respect for the land and the people.

WISTO Studio
Chongqing, Yubei District

Client: WISTO
Type: organic farming and kitchen

Size: 2,000 m²
Year: 2015

Studio Organic Farming The concept of 'Half-farming and Half-X' is alive and in practice at WISTO's studio space. The courtyard and roof terraces of the premises are designated for urban farming. The organic farming group, a team of around thirty members of WISTO's staff,

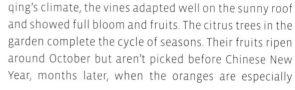

takes care of the gardens. Collectively, they dedicate their spare time in the evening and on weekends to farm together. The group discusses the plant selection and arrangements, they prepare the soil and planting beds in spring, maintain the fields throughout the summer months and harvest and tidy up before winter. Organic compost methods are studied and tested in the garden. It is a work in progress. With each passing year, the skills and knowledge of the team advances and the fruits of their shared efforts become richer. The garden has so far yielded vegetables such as green beans, cucumbers, tomatoes, peppers, aubergines, and leeks. Passionfruit vines from Guilin, the hometown one of the founder, are the newest arrival on the rooftop. Uncommon in Chong-

qing's climate, the vines adapted well on the sunny roof and showed full bloom and fruits. The citrus trees in the garden complete the cycle of seasons. Their fruits ripen around October but aren't picked before Chinese New Year, months later, when the oranges are especially

sweet. Rapeseed is sawn on the first day of frost each year and everyone gather for lunch in the garden to watch the explosion of colour in the courtyard in spring. The harvest of the garden is shared with the team and guests. Fruits and vegetables are offered at the company's front desk every day and the staff are encouraged to 'steal their dish', taking ingredients for home cooking from the garden. Besides the daily catering, the office kitchen prepares organic dishes on special occasions for studio guests and friends. Once a year, WISTO arranges a studio Family Day, when everyone brings along their children for a day of fun and learning. The children are invited to explore the garden, pick fruits and vegetables and carry their 'harvest' home with the family.

184

Village of Return

Guiyuan Town, Wulong County

Client: Found Vision Ltd.
Type: resort design, farmland restoration

Size: 50,000 m²
Year: 2017

Place Guiyuan town is located in Xiannv Mountain in Wulong county to the east of Chongqing. The mountain range forms part of the Wulong Karst National Geology Park, a UNESCO World Heritage site famous for its caves and natural bridges and Qingkou Tiankeng, one of the largest sinkholes in the world, formed by surface water. The new hotel and resort complex is situated on a small 60-hectare plateau at an altitude of 1,100 meters, a pastoral enclave bordered by dramatic mountain cliffs. The entire holiday village is planned to encompass seven areas of bespoke accommodation and leisure facilities. To date, the Wild Luxury Resort, the Children's Farm and B&B, and the Cultural and Creative Industries area have been completed, while the Tiankeng Wonders, the Discovery Forest and the Holiday Community are under construction.

Approach WISTO's design thinking stems from three angles: the people, the land and the scenery and the intent to create a place in resonance with all three aspects. This project is no exception. Yet the stakes were unexpectedly high. "We found a breathtaking landscape and unique scenery which stood in striking contrast to the village in decline and the sense of alienation of the local people from the land. The old farmhouse was in decay. The pastures were left abandoned. After several visits and rounds of discussions, we finally felt we had found the key: the idea of reinvigorating people's interaction with the land and its richness became the source of the design and defining criteria of all programmes."

Design The resort design started with the renovation of the old farmstead and the refurbishment of the adjacent outdoor areas. In parallel, the design team of WISTO, working closely with the Taiwan Taichung Peace Agriculture Association, researched organic farming methods suitable to revive the pastures. Due to the geomorphology of the karst, the soil of the basin is meagre.

The overuse of chemical fertiliser for extended tobacco plantations had additionally deteriorated the condition of the soil. Tibetan gesang flowers (Cosmos bipinnatus), spider flowers (Cleome hassleriana) and rapeseed were sown across the plateau and used as green manure to gradually regenerate the topsoil layer.

The low rock walls zigzagging across the steep hills were restored. The cornfields on the man-made terraces are tiny and their corn production is low, yet the quality of the crops is surprisingly high, with the corn particularly sweet and flavourful. On the plateau, the original network of irrigation channels was repaired, and supplementary water tanks installed. Today, the stormwater once again rushes through the fields in the wet season and children play along the rock lines when the rain has gone. Lastly, highbush blueberries were planted. The berries are well-suited to the altitude of the plateau, as they can tolerate poor soil conditions and require low year-round temperatures. Today, the corn and berries are sold as specialty products of the valley.

In addition, bamboo, as the most commonly used natural material in the region, caught the designers' attention. Bamboo rafts, baskets, fences, and adobe houses reinforced with bamboo canes are omnipresent in the valley and local farmers familiar with every aspect of bamboo weaving and construction. Hence, WISTO invited the farmers to contribute to the project with their craftsmanship. The farmers erected all bamboo fences at the resort and supported the designers with their knowledge when testing and building the project's bamboo structures.

Since completion, the project has won various awards acknowledging the design as well as its sustainable and community-based approach. As WISTO summarises the value of the project: "Observing the ingenuity of local farmers and sharing moments of pride and joy in the joint accomplishment has been the most rewarding part of the work."

Karst cliffs and pastoral enclave – sustainable resort village design ››

Old and new – restored farmhouse lobby and panorama restaurant
Local limestone paving – Tibetan gesang flower meadows

Resort villas – nestled in the mountain topography

Muted colour scheme – local materials and landscape integration

Bamboo weave ^

Community Barn shared by villagers and guests – a resting place and nature education outdoor classroom ⌄

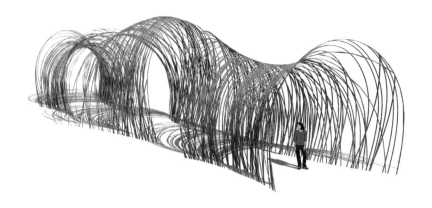

^ Bamboo cane studies

∨ Tea Pavilion – a community space for tea sharing and a fireplace for cool mountain evenings

Reading Pavilion ⌃

Bamboo canopy and limestone seating ⌄

Mountain trails ›

Villa path ›

Longfor Island
Chongqing, Bishan District

Client: Longfor Group Holdings Ltd.
Type: arrival plaza, clubhouse courtyard

Size: 8,000 m²
Year: 2019

Place Longfor Island is a recent large-scale residential development in Lyudao New Area, Bishan district, Chongqing. Formerly a county, Bishan became a municipal district of Chongqing in 2014 and a key area of Chongqing's western urban expansion. Named after 'the white stone from the mountain, transparent and smooth like jade,' Bishan is an ancient township established during the Tang dynasty, rich in legends and historical connotations, and known as 'a place to let one's thoughts wander'.

Approach Since the late 1990s, various styles have predominated in Chinese real estate design, from European style to Southeast Asian style and New-China style, culminating in the current Neoclassical Asian style most prominent in high-end residential developments across China. Starting from the interior design of the promotion centres of the new estates, the Neoclassical Asian style extended into the landscape design of the arrival areas and courtyard design of the display villas, becoming the most sought-after residential landscape style in China in recent years. While impeccable in its construction quality and overall character setting, the new style tends to be less discerning in the selection of motifs and layouts applied. Generous combinations of iconic Asian features in landscape design characterise most neoclassical gardens, ranging from Japanese traditional landscape elements such as stone lanterns, bonsai pine, dry landscapes, stunning deer, to European influences, as in soft outdoor furniture, lavish flower arrangements, large-scale bronze sculptures, and Southeast Asian references such as flower boats and shiny water droplets. At Longfor Island, WISTO seeks alternative ways to recall the atmosphere of classical Chinese landscape gardens in a modern living environment.

Design The design refrains from using decorative objects and features and instead focuses on the character and experience of the place by recreating iconic traditional garden scenes in a pure and minimalist manner. Greys and greens and minimalist flower scenes define the design of the arrival plaza and courtyards of the display villas, depicting poetic scenes of life in the mountains. A large canopy structure weaving around a sky well greets the guests at the entrance of the court. The composition refers to traditional Sishui Guitang residences, where rainwater was collected in the patio of the buildings, creating a commodity beneficial to all residents. Evoking a sense of Sishui Guitang living, visitors are welcomed into an area of comfort and tranquillity under the shelter of the roof. The shape of the canopy derives from the allegory of the reflection of a crescent moon on water. The perspective lines of the floating roof create the illusion of silhouettes of hills and clouds. The pillars of the canopy are spaced in alignment with the gently curving roof, denser at the core where screening the view towards the garden, and more widely spaced alongside the water feature.

The outdoor corridor continues alongside a flight of cascading water, taking advantage of the three-metre level difference on site. Beginning from a silent pond on the highest plateau, the water flows gently down the mound. Rhythmically orchestrated by ripple effects and overflows, the sound of the cascading water recalls the sound of creeks in the mountains, creating the soothing atmosphere recorded in Chinese poetry: 'The quieter the cicada chirps, the more secluded the bird sings.'

In the words of WISTO: "The design celebrates the peacefulness of water, whether static or dynamic, quiet or vocal. All occurrences of water are ever pleasant."

At the upper pond, three sculptural pine trees encircle a tranquil islet in the water. They set the stage for the final allegory implied in the journey from garden entrance to reception hall: 'Washing the inkstone near the tree by the river, ink floating on the water like flowers blooming and appearing.'

Floating roof and cascading water ››

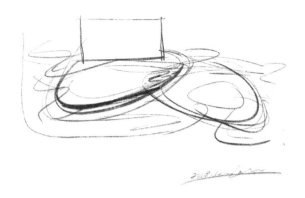

Interlacing shapes

‹‹ Dialogue of
roof and water ›

Floating canopy

‹‹ Silhouettes of hills
and clouds

Screened views and
sequenced arrival experience ›

Bamboo forest
‹‹ Arrival courtyard
Villa paths ›

Freedom Tree House
Qiyun Mountain, Anhui Province

Client: Freedom House
Type: resort design, landscape planning

Size: 13,000 m²
Year: 2019

Place Mount Qiyun is located in Xiuning county in southern Anhui province and known as one of the Four Sacred Mountains of Taoism. Surrounded by clouds year-round, the scenery is unparalleled, resembling an ink painting. Nestled in the pine forests of Qiyunshan National Geological Park, Freedom Treehouse caters to discerning guests seeking a holiday destination immersed in nature and isolated from the outside world.

Approach "When we first came to this mountain forest and absorbed the splendour of the scenery, we immediately thought about how to protect its natural beauty. We wanted to create a place that looked as if it were emerging from the forest, rather than being imposed upon it. A place and experience visitors will deeply and wholeheartedly remember." This initial impression and design objective of WISTO perfectly corresponded with the design intent of the owner of the resort, who aimed for a unique nature retreat. WISTO became the lead consultant of the project team of architecture and interior design firms and their landscape-based approach to site planning the guideline throughout all project stages.

Design At first, a comprehensive site survey was conducted covering the physical parameters of the terrain such as slope conditions, sun aspects and vegetation coverage as well as a visual impact assessment study – including a catalogue of 'memory points', as WISTO terms them, identifying viewpoints and memorable landscape scenes. Based on the survey data the site layout and location of the villas were determined, granting optimal panoramic views for each villa and hotel room. All villas and leisure decks are built on pillars, with each building footprint confined to 40 to 80 square meters to preserve the uninterrupted canopy of pine trees and to minimise the buildings' impact on the well-established shrub and groundcover layers of the terrain. The steep slopes of the site were kept intact,

and elevated boardwalks introduced to connect the villas and resort facilities, at-grade where possible. A secondary trail system at ground level allows for further exploration of the forest areas.

Additionally, a set of recreational decks punctuates the forest. The multi-level outdoor facilities connect the elevated walkway system with the forest paths. They provide leisure destinations for families and groups, sheltered from the sun throughout the day and open towards the sky for stargazing at night. In conjunction with the family decks, children's play facilities are integrated into the platforms. Climbing nets span between the platforms and spiral down to the lower levels, encouraging children to explore the forest at various elevations and to test and challenge their motor skills in a fun, yet safe manner. Rattan domes, similar to the bamboo structures in the Village of Return provide semi-shade for the children's decks. The lightweight structures are constructed from steel frames with rattan weave, creating the transparent vaults.

Opened in autumn 2019, the resort attracted nationwide attention from the design profession and tourism industry alike, setting a new benchmark for nature integration into resort design in China.

Qiyun Mountain – Freedom Tree House main building ››

Children's play and leisure decks punctuating the forest canopy ^

Forest play
<< Climbing decks
Treasure cabins >

Canyon of Light
Meishan, Sichuan Province

Client: Sunac China Holdings Ltd.
Type: arrival plaza, residential design

Size: 18,000 m²
Year: 2019

Place The project is located in Shigao town in Meishan city, Renshou county. The area forms part of Chengdu's thriving Tianfu New District economic zone and is designated for mixed-use development. The new residential compound has a total planned area of 12.5 hectares.

Approach WISTO was commissioned to design the entrance sequence of the new residential estate along the northern perimeter of the site. The 320-metre-long strip of land projected as the future welcome area revealed itself as a jigsaw puzzle of infrastructure elements and haphazard elevation changes. The main road bordering the site gradually ascends towards a viaduct to the east. A high-voltage line borders the road, flanked by a steep slope at an incline of 25 to 35% that mitigates the levels between the road and the lower-lying site. Rising up to a nine-metre difference in height at the viaduct, the widening slope halves the available landscape area of the entrance corridor. The floor levels of the future buildings are set independently from the gradients of the terrain, leading to a rapid level drop at the arrival building and up to ten-metre-tall retaining walls, where the basement is exposed. With site conditions far from ideal for an inviting welcome gesture and pleasant arrival experience for future residents, WISTO's initial questioning of the site's character led to unexpected results. "How can such a broken venue be healed? How to transform inherent weaknesses into positive features that create a brand-new space and an experience, so as to become the uniqueness, recognition, and aesthetic value of the project itself? With this thinking in mind, we started to disentangle the puzzle."

Design The Canyon of Light became the defining feature of the pedestrian arrival experience. The naturally shaped walls of the canyon not only effectively shield the outer wires and retaining walls, but also create a poetic passage through light and shadow. Moulded like a mountain gorge, the canyon recreates an artistic expression of nature against the backdrop of the uniform and nondescript city fabric all around.

Observing the visitors, WISTO describes the new experience as such: "Under the light of the sky, some people are silent, others are thinking. The light slowly flows with time. In the morning, noon and evening, sunlight and starlight become the true artists in this space. Their rays of light penetrate through the darkness. At the tortuous turning point of the two black flowing walls, a 'vacuum of darkness' arises, making people instantly feel isolated from the outside world. Perhaps in this moment of darkness, we may see the light within ourselves instead. Another light. The sunlight streaming through the openings in the wall, sacred, clear, pure, and striking. In light, there is the power of life. When the willow blossoms. At the end of the tunnel, the still water surface of the bay reflects the sky and clouds. A moment of self-questioning, standing silently in the sunlight."

Any aesthetic vision in design can only be realised in tune with technology, as WISTO points out. All throughout the process, from design to implementation, the team of WISTO worked closely with structural engineers and manufacturers to develop a structural frame for the natural stone cladding, technically sound and cost-efficient, yet visually unnoticeable.

Arrival experience – Canyon of Light ››

Site condition – a jigsaw puzzle of elevations and infrastructure lines ˄

"Under the light of the sky, some people are silent, others are thinking. The light slowly flows with time. In the morning, noon and evening, sunlight and starlight become the true artists in this space. Their rays of light penetrate through the darkness. At the tortuous turning point of the two black flowing walls, a 'vacuum of darkness' arises, making people instantly feel isolated from the outside world. Perhaps in this moment of darkness, we may see the light within ourselves instead. Another light. The sunlight streaming through the openings in the wall, sacred, clear, pure, and striking. In light, there is the power of life. When the willow blossoms. At the end of the tunnel, the still water surface of the bay reflects the sky and clouds. A moment of self-questioning, standing silently in the sunlight."

Clover Nature School

Grassroots Urban Regeneration

Shanghai

Clover Nature School

Shanghai

Founder: Liu Yuelai, Wei Min, Fan Haoyang
Founded: 2014
Team: 20–45
Location: Shanghai
Portfolio: permaculture, community gardens, urban farming, community building, outreach programmes, environmental training

Clover Nature School is a non-profit organisation concerned with environmental practice and education based at Tongji University in Shanghai. Founded in 2014 by Liu Yuelai, Wei Min and Fan Haoyang, the team today consists of thirty members of staff with diverse professional backgrounds, ranging from landscape architecture to social work, urban cultural studies, urban planning and ecology. Clover Nature School's mission and community engagement strategy is based upon four pillars: ecological design, community building, environmental management and educational training.

Starting from two urban permaculture gardens, built and managed by Clover Nature School – the Nature Line Garden and the Knowledge & Innovation Community Garden – the initiative has evolved into a wide network of community gardens in co-governance and self-governance. Urban gardeners have started greening the city. They are spreading Clover's ethos through multiplier effects across Shanghai, making Clover Nature School's vision of a 'participatory, co-built, urban wonderland at everybody's doorstep' gradually become a Shanghai reality.

In addition, Clover Nature School's advocacy for sustainable grassroots city regeneration has gained nationwide attention. Clover's expertise and practice experience in community building and co-governance is widely shared at conferences, and local government leaders as well as national and international experts are regular visitors to the project sites. With resilient inner-city renewal high on the urban agenda in China, the grassroots initiative by Clover Nature School in Shanghai is bound to take root in cities across China.

In conversation with Liu Yuelai, Fan Haoyang and Wei Min about simplicity and ideals, community gardens as urban catalysts, and resilience.

Clover Nature School in Shanghai is an exceptional landscape practice in China focussing on grassroots community engagement and environmental education. Your practice, projects and conferences changed the professional discourse in many ways. How did it all start?

Liu Yuelai 2014, the year we started Clover Nature School, was an exceptional year. Many experts call it 'the founding year of nature education in

Liu Yuelai is the President of Clover Nature School and Director of the Experimental Centre of Community Gardens and Community Empowerment at Tongji University, Shanghai. Liu Yuelai holds a Ph.D. in Landscape Architecture from the College of Architecture and Urban Planning at Tongji University, Shanghai. Taking environmental design and education as a cue for sustainable city development, he actively promotes participatory design and self-organisation through community gardens. A pioneer in the field of community co-governance, Liu Yuelai leads the discourse on community building and public participation in the Shanghai metropolis and beyond.

Wei Min is the Vice-President of Clover Nature School. She holds a Ph.D. in Architecture from the College of Architecture and Urban Planning at Tongji University, Shanghai. Wei Min is a Class 1 Registered Architect (PRC) and a certified teacher of permaculture. With her expertise in spatial design and natural systems, Wei Min is an advocate of cross-disciplinary design and manages the participatory trajectories and environmental education programmes of Clover Nature School.

Fan Haoyang is the Managing Director of Clover Nature School. He holds a Bachelor of Architecture from the College of Architecture and Urban Planning at Tongji University, Shanghai. Fan Haoyang is a Class 1 Registered Architect (PRC) and a Registered Urban and Rural Planner. Prior Clover Nature School, Fan Haoyang co-founded and directed Pandscape, an office focused on environmental planning and design in Shanghai, in collaboration with Liu Yuelai.

‹‹ Biodiversity Volunteer Team documentary – *Resupinatus*, Tricholomataceae, fungi

Liu Yuelai (l.), Wei Min (c.), Fan Haoyang (r.) – Clover Nature School team ››

China'. New environmental education institutes and programmes kicked off across the country. Even the term 'nature education' was invented that year and is now used by everyone. From the beginning of Clover Nature School, we intended to combine environmental training and awareness with community building. Our focus at that time and still today is on the participation of children through nature education.

Fan Haoyang All three of us are graduates from the College of Architecture and Urban Planning (CAUP) at Tongji University in Shanghai. In 2010 Liu Yuelai and I started Pandscape together, a practice concerned with environmental design and focused on small-scale projects. Later, when Wei Min joined us with her background in permaculture, we established Clover Nature School to connect nature education and community engagement with sustainable design for the city.

I understood the Chinese name of Clover Nature School differs from the English, in which respect?

Fan Haoyang We actually call it four-leaf clover in Chinese. The plant is special as it is the result of meiosis. It is not an ordinary part of nature. In fact, it has a unique and magical existence in nature. And it is fun.

Liu Yuelai The Chinese name is Si Ye (Clover) Caotang. Caotang literally means 'thatched roof'. In ancient China literati used to call their study hall Caotang. Tang dynasty poets such as Bai Juyi (772–846) and Du Fu (712–770) had their thatched cottages at Mount Lu, Jiangxi province and in the outskirts of Chengdu in Sichuan province respectively, where one can still visit the reconstruction of the original Du Fu Thatched Cottage and also Wang Wei (699–759) is praised. The Caotang represents culture, education and its spiritual connotation. It is a simple and understated name, yet also austere, and the composed Chinese character contains 'grass' and hence provides a reference to nature. As our logo Clover Caotang means luck, it carries an ideal and it is a place for education.

Wei Min We all have children. When I joined Clover Nature School, my daughter was two years old. I think it is important for children to be close to nature and to have the chance to discover and engage in natural processes in a playful way. In Shanghai, there is hardly any

We actually call it four-leaf clover in Chinese. The plant is special as it is the result of meiosis. It is not an ordinary part of nature. In fact, it has a unique and magical existence in nature. As our logo Clover Caotang means luck, it carries an ideal and it is a place for education.

210

natural environment left in the city anymore. It is all developed land stretching for kilometres from the city centre to the periphery. As designers, we can recreate nature in the city and help all children experience nature again close to their homes. Especially now in this year of the pandemic, when we are intensively discussing the interference of humans with the natural environment.

As you mentioned the pandemic, how did it affect Clover Nature School's work?

Liu Yuelai Our mission never stops, but we needed to adjust our means. In spring, we started an online initiative called 'seeding'. We had launched the 'Shanghai Blooming Action' in the past years aiming to establish 2040 community gardens in Shanghai by the year 2040. Yet without any seeding, there is no blooming. During this special spring period, when everyone was at home, we encouraged residents to green their balconies using the abundance of newly gained spare time for productive activities like planting, composting and collecting seedlings. As always, this action was not only about 'planting' but also about establishing connections between neighbours, while physical contact wasn't in the picture. In addition to the online platform, we used post-its on walls or seedling-letters to spread the word in the neighbourhoods. We also created a small device we called the 'mini seed ark', a small basket where everyone put seeds inside. Later, people hung the 'mini seed ark' on a tree so that people passing-by could pick-up the seeds and join the action on their balconies. When public life returns, everyone can come together again and plant their seedlings in the community gardens. It is very simple. It can be easily done nationwide. Within the first two weeks of our 'seeding' event, over 200 people in Shanghai had participated.

To what extent is the combination of city greening and social interaction a recurring objective in Clover Nature School's events?

Liu Yuelai It is actually the main point. The epidemic is only an extreme situation creating loneliness and isolation, but it is certainly not the only one. When you adopt a seedling, you adopt life. The seedling represents hope, the giving creates mutual help. This kindness is needed in all of life's circumstances, not only now.

When you adopt a seedling, you adopt life. The seedling represents hope, the giving creates mutual help. This kindness is needed in all of life's circumstances.

Compared to community gardens in the West, do you experience a difference in approach or acceptance in China?

Wei Min I think to a large extent it is the same. Around the globe, community gardens are about connecting people, improving the environment in the city and sharing knowledge about permaculture principles in planting and composting. It is about a greener life, which is especially important in high-density cities in China and elsewhere.

Liu Yuelai To add to Wei Min's point, our community gardens follow two objectives: one is urban agriculture and another the environmentally-friendly greening of the city. A metropolis like Shanghai needs green spaces and landscaping. In China, landscape aesthetics are still evolving. Years back, it was all about purely decorative green. Today everyone pays more attention to urban ecologies and the improvement of the environment. But still, applying permaculture principles within a high-density urban setting where public space is a rare good requires more emphasis on aesthetics to make ecological gardens acceptable to all.

Fan Haoyang One difference might be that our community gardens address a broad audience. It is less about a 'special interest' group and far more about building a wider community, including all age groups and encouraging social interaction in the neighbourhoods.

Could you provide an example of Clover Nature School's collaboration with neighbourhood initiatives?

Wei Min Baicao Garden in Yangpu district, for example, started with a group of elderly citizens who were interested in urban gardening. They approached the district council, who engaged us to facilitate the setup of the garden. It was the first community garden in Yangpu district in co-governance with Clover Nature School. Today there are many more. Baicao Garden occupies a quarter of a small pocket park and is quite exposed. Over the years, more and more families gained interest in the gardening group. The neighbourhood initiative is still growing. The group maintains the garden and we support the gardeners in management issues and communication. We organise events and training, but also open forums where everyone gets together to discuss current 'issues',

Today everyone pays more attention to urban ecologies and the improvement of the environment. But still, applying permaculture principles within a high-density urban setting where public space is a rare good requires more emphasis on aesthetics to make ecological gardens acceptable to all.

Clover Nature School – 四叶草堂 Four-leaf Grass Cottage – 四叶草 Four-leaf Clover – 草堂 Thatched Cottage – 草 Grass ᴧ

such as the funding of new plants and tools, but also the theft of such, which unfortunately still occurs.

Liu Yuelai The different age groups are an important aspect in our work. Projects such as Baicao Garden are partially funded by the district government, which is engaging us as an NGO to support the community groups. At those community gardens, the elderly indeed form a large part of the participants. Most of them are retirees, they have time to spare and are interested in gathering and sharing. It is also worth mentioning that they grew up in an era before China's rapid urbanisation; like the residents of Puxing Road, for example, who joined a permaculture training at Clover Nature School. During their youth, this area was farmland which they cultivated together with their parents. Later, the area turned from agricultural fields into a mixed-use urban district. But the old community still lives there. Also, today's retirees belong to the age bracket of the generation of the 'Up to the Mountains and Down to the Countryside Movement' during the Great Leap Forward, when the so-called privileged urban youth was sent to the countryside. In a nutshell, many older citizens are familiar with farming methods and are happy to expand their knowledge into ecological urban farming. Today, they bring their grandchildren with them and enjoy gardening together across generations. Other projects like the 'Shanghai Blooming Action' are more directed towards a young urban crowd concerned with a greener city, health and sustainable living.

As a pioneer in the field of community participation in China, how did you spread Clover's mission both locally in Shanghai and beyond?

Liu Yuelai Indeed, our team in Shanghai were pioneers in this field in China. We studied, tested and applied many methods of social governance in our projects from various levels of co-governance to outreach programmes and self-governance, which made our mission continuously grow and diversify. Clover's community gardens are not simply places for urban gardening, but places for people to connect and to initiate social responsibility. In the open forums Wei Min mentioned, we also discuss issues beyond the singular gardens, like the planning and development of the neighbourhood, directly with the local community. Also, our ideas are spreading. Similar initiatives are now happening in many major large

Clover's community gardens are not simply places for urban gardening, but places for people to connect and to initiate social responsibility.

214

and medium-sized cities across the country. At the moment, the Shanghai initiative is still the strongest, but there's a network around which is constantly expanding. Clover Nature School is based at Tongji University, where I head the Experimental Centre of Community Gardens and Community Empowerment. This connection between practice and academic discourse is vital to our work. In 2019, for example, we organised the first national community garden conference in Shanghai, with 300 participants from all different provinces and international speakers including Shin Aiba from Tokyo Metropolitan University, Jeffrey Hou from Washington University in Seattle, Helen Wooley from Sheffield University and Ryo Yamazaki from studio-L, Japan.

Wei Min I think sharing is key both locally and nationally and even internationally. We have many experts visiting our projects each year, practitioners as well as academics. We also arrange a wide array of events where everyone in the community is invited to partake, from fruit-picking or outdoor evening reading classes at the KIC Garden to specialist groups like the Biodiversity Volunteer Group.

What is your outlook? What will be the next steps in Clover's Nature School's public engagement?

Liu Yuelai Clover Nature School has been working on community participation and urban regeneration in Shanghai for six years now. We have had our initial failures and successes, and we are still working on making Clover's mission more sustainable and profound. I personally think the pandemic has taught us a lesson as well – a lesson about resilience. Everyone's ultimate autonomy lies in their own resilience. How can everyone strengthen their own resistance? How can everyone take care of their own body and mind to be more energetic and powerful – not just with respect to health but to their wider personal life? In fact, in the profession the term 'resilience' is mainly aimed at city design. How to build resilient cities? In our opinion, it starts from the resilience of each individual and their families and spreads further to the neighbourhoods, the wider community, the districts and finally changes the city. Resilience derives from each individual's state of mind, from sharing and building up networks, and we as Clover Nature School will contribute to this process the best we can.

How to build resilient cities? In our opinion, it starts from the resilience of each individual and their families and spreads further to the neighbourhoods, the wider community, the districts and finally changes the city. Resilience derives from each individual's state of mind, from sharing and building up networks.

KIC Community Garden
Shanghai, Yangpu District

Funding: Yangpu Science and Technology Innovation Group, Shui On Land

Size: 2,000 m²
Year: since 2016

Place The Knowledge & Innovation Community Garden (KICG) is Clover Nature School's prime learning and community centre, established in 2016. It forms an integral part of the Knowledge & Innovation Community (KIC) business park in Yangpu district, Shanghai. Jointly developed by the Yangpu district government and Shui On Land property company, KIC business park is home to Fudan University, Tongji University and Shanghai University of Finance and Economics, next to over one hundred scientific research institutions. Under the tenet of 'Innovation, Entrepreneurship, LOHAS – Building Shanghai's Think-Tank', KIC seeks to connect the spirit of scientific innovation with entrepreneurship, collaboration and sustainable living through a culture of open-source knowledge.

Approach Clover Nature School aims to spread the vision of KIC beyond the newly established business park into the adjacent residential neighbourhoods, turning the experience of nature and environmental learning into an integral part of daily life. A vacant lot surrounded by residential communities and earmarked by Yangpu Science and Technology Innovation Group and Shui On Land for redevelopment into a public park offered a unique window of opportunity to kickstart Clover Nature School's grassroots initiative. Built and funded by the Shui On Group and operated and maintained by Clover Nature School, the Knowledge & Innovation Community Garden (KICG) became the first public community garden project in Shanghai and a pivotal project for Clover's mission of sustainable urban regeneration through community parks and gardens.

Programme The Knowledge & Innovation Community Garden (KICG) is designed as an urban farm and ecological laboratory. The diverse sections of the garden are dedicated to sustainable agriculture, habitat restoration, nature experience and outdoor classroom facilities.

The sky-blue shipping container at the centre of the site houses the learning centre. It announces the project from afar. Inside, the Community Living Room serves tea and coffee to regular guests and passers-by alike. Dried flowers, part of the seed library and the plant identification system of the facility, decorate the walls. Workshops and training are held either here or in the adjacent outdoor classroom square. The educational programmes of KICG range from children, respective parent-child, learning and playing activities, to nature observation classes and advanced multi-day courses in permaculture and urban farming. Reading classes expand the park programme into the evening hours. Regular community events such as fruit picking and farmers markets, and seasonal festivals further strengthen ties with the neighbouring communities. The public urban farming area to the east of the park is designed as a cooperative cultivation experiment. Participants are invited to claim one of the thirty-eight 1-by-1-metre planting beds to grow their favourite fruits and vegetables, while professional instructors offer guidance on sustainable agriculture and natural fertilising methods. A small adjacent greenhouse provides seedlings for the miniature farming lots. In addition, spiral herb gardens, keyhole gardens, banana circles and sheet mulch gardens next to the participatory fields showcase advanced organic farming techniques. The western area of KICG is dedicated to nature experience and ecological learning. Various habitats from seasonal ponds to dry gardens and wetland biotopes are established here. The small gardens are funded by landscape companies' donations and private sponsorship. In the four years since its establishment, the Knowledge & Innovation Community Garden (KICG) has not only been embraced by the local community but recognised by district government departments as a benchmark project for community building, social engagement and environmental learning.

Knowledge & Innovation Community Garden and Learning Centre ››

‹ Observing the city through the lens of Clover – a child in search of nature play.

KICG provides a place for this quest to connect with nature in the city.

Rice planting event at KICG – combining children learning and fun ⌄

"Today is Father's Day. Grandfather, father and I go to KICG to learn about rice planting" ›

‹ Environmental learning

‹ Evening reading classes

Fruit-picking event ›

Farmers markets ›

Nature Line Garden

Shanghai, Baoshan District

Funding: Elite Valley Ltd.
Type: permaculture, research and education

Size: 4,700 m²
Year: since 2015

Place The Nature Line Garden is the result of a conversion of a typical terrain vague in the city into a permaculture education centre. The narrow, 400-metre long strip of land owned by Elite Valley, a creative industry park in Baoshan district in the northern metropolitan area of Shanghai, was originally planned as a green buffer between the Shanghai-Wusong railway line and Jungong Road, a major district thoroughfare. Over the years, the neglected and barely maintained urban interstice became a dumping ground for construction waste, next to local residents' informal vegetable gardens.

Approach Nature education stands at the core of Clover Nature School's mission. The forgotten land along the railway tracks provided an exceptional opportunity to realise the first permaculture garden in the metropolitan area of Shanghai. With the support of Elite Valley, who granted the land and funding for the construction of the permaculture garden, Clover developed the Nature Line Garden as a research facility and education centre. Clover Nature School's permaculture design certificate (PDC) training courses are held here. Now in its fifth year, Nature Line Garden has become a popular natural classroom for the district's primary and middle schools and the students of Tongji University alike.

Programme The elongated shape of the site allowed for a prototypical layout, in accordance with the five classic zones of permaculture established by Bill Mollison and David Holmgren. Organised according to the frequency of human use and plants or animal needs, the five zones are laid out consecutively, starting from the highly frequented education centre towards the undisturbed wilderness zone at the eastern tip of the site.
Zone 0, at the entrance to the site, supports the highest level of human activity. Workshops and seminars are held in the learning centre in this zone. Research is conducted here, and maintenance equipment stored.

Zone 1, where herbs and vegetables are grown, encircles the built facilities of zone 0. Rainwater is harvested for irrigation and the water cycle mechanism displayed for children for interactive learning. Kitchen waste is composted in vermicompost units.
The westernmost extension of the site was selected to showcase zone 2. The 1-by-1-metre perennial gardens and semi-intensive orchards structure this area.
The low-interference permaculture zones 3 to 5 line the tracks towards the east, with each compartment gradually decreasing in scheduled maintenance frequency. The sequence of crop fields and tree plantations ends with the unmanaged wilderness zone at the most remote eastern end of the site. Cut off from the surrounding urban fabric and shielded from human intervention, the biodiversity is richest here.

Biodiversity Volunteer Group Habitat protection and biodiversity conservation are two of Clover Nature School's key research trajectories. Beginning in 2018, Clover collaborated with The Nature Conservancy (TNC), under whose scientific guidance the seasonal ponds of KICG and the remote areas of the Nature Line Garden were transformed into demonstration areas, and habitat monitoring activities were launched. After undergoing specialised training, the Biodiversity Volunteer Group, formed by community garden members, conducts and records long-term observations at KICG and the Nature Line Garden. As of September 2018, 142 species of plants (including 31 native species) and 21 species of animals could be found in the KIC Garden, and 172 species of plants (including 52 species of native plants) and 32 species of animals were documented in the Nature Line Garden.

Charaxes bernardus, Nymphalidae, tawny rajah
Permaculture zoning map
Mustela sibirica, Mustelidae, Siberian weasel
Nature Line Garden – zone 3 ››

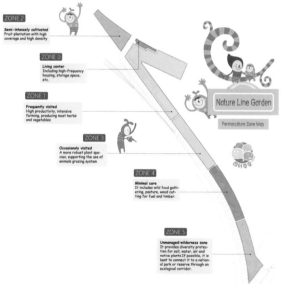

ZONE 2
Semi-intensely cultivated
Fruit plantation with high coverage and high density

ZONE 0
Living center
Including high-frequency housing, storage space, etc.

ZONE 1
Frequently visited
High productivity, intensive farming, producing most herbs and vegetables

ZONE 3
Occasionaly visited
A more robust plant species, supporting the use of animals grazing system

ZONE 4
Minimal care
It includes wild food gathering, pasture, wood cutting for fuel and timber

ZONE 5
Unmanaged:wilderness zone
It provides diversity protection for soil, water, air and native plants.If possible, it is best to connect it to a national park or reserve through an ecological corridor.

Nature Line Garden

Permaculture Zone Map

<< *Dictyoglomus*
Dictyoglomaceae
bacterium

<< *Hierodula patellifera*
Mantidae
praying mantis

Cryptotympana atrata ›
Cicadidae
cicada

<< *Schizophyllum commune*
Schizophyllaceae
fungi

<< *Cyathus stercoreus*
Nidulariaceae
bird's nest fungi

Auricularia ›
Auriculariaceae
jelly fungi

<< *Oxyopes sertatus*
Oxyopidae
lynx spider

<< *Ruspolia lineosa*
Tettigoniidae
bush cricket

Armadillidium vulgare ›
Armadillidiidae
woodlouse

Community Gardens

Shanghai, Yangpu District

Funding: Yangpu District Government Size: varies
Type: co-governance, urban renewal Year: since 2016

Place Since the beginning of the twenty-first century, the economy of the Yangpu district has shifted away from labour-intensive industry, towards commerce and advanced technologies. Today, the Knowledge & Innovation Community (KIC) business park at the heart of Yangpu district is one of Shanghai's leading knowledge and innovation cluster.

Nonetheless, the old residential quarters neighbouring KIC and dating from the 1950s to the 1990s are time-worn and the area's public spaces in decay. Green civic squares are sparse, and their planting palettes and layouts standardised. By contrast, the layout of the residential estates shows an abundance of communal green space. However, with maintenance costs high and the focus of urban planning during the past decades set on city expansion and new developments rather than the upkeep of the existing inner-city urban fabric, the appearance of the residential green spaces faded and left them underutilised today.

Approach The open spaces of the elder estates suffer from what Liu Yuelai terms 'aesthetic fatigue'. While green spaces are present in sufficient quantities, a lack of care has lessened their quality leading to an artificial shortage of usable public urban green areas, with adverse effects on the local neighbourhood's liveability. The community garden programme launched by Clover Nature School therefore addresses both ecological renewal and community building through civic participation. Organised in co-governance with neighbourhood committees and residents, the community gardens give citizens the opportunity to contribute directly to the improvement of their living environment and the city's wider ecological renewal.

Clover Nature School helps the grassroots initiatives progress by providing permaculture knowledge as well as guidance in site management through monitoring and mediation. Open forums are regularly organised at the Baicao community garden for all urban gardeners to discuss immediate challenges and concerns as well as future aspirations.

In the past five years, sixty community gardens have been established in Yangpu district and beyond. The emerging grassroots network of urban gardeners gained the attention and growing support of district governments at various levels for offering a bottom-up solution to the pressing task of sustainable urban renewal in the inner-city quarters of Shanghai.

As Clover Nature School concludes: "Grassroots urban renovation is a tentative experiment, which requires gradual exploration. It can only succeed with the support of all parties involved: participating, co-operating, and sharing their thoughts and expertise. The community building approach we currently employ is based on case-by-case experience and extensive participation. Unavoidably, there have been 'troubles' in the management and operation of the gardens. Yet we believe that exactly these 'troubles' will lead to an even more conscious motivation and immanent strength of the communities."

Programme The community gardens vary in scale and location, ranging from small green enclaves collaboratively built and maintained by residents of the adjacent housing blocks to subdivisions of pocket parks under the co-management of neighbourhood committees.

All community gardens are built upon permaculture principles, including rainwater harvesting, ecological composting, spiral herb gardens, vegetable fields and fruit trees.

All gardens are non-profit, with seedlings, trees and material supply funded by donations. The volunteer gardeners include people of all age groups, from community elders – who enjoy sharing their farming knowledge from times prior to China's rapid urbanisation – to young urbanites and families with children.

Community gardens in Yangpu district and beyond – location map ››

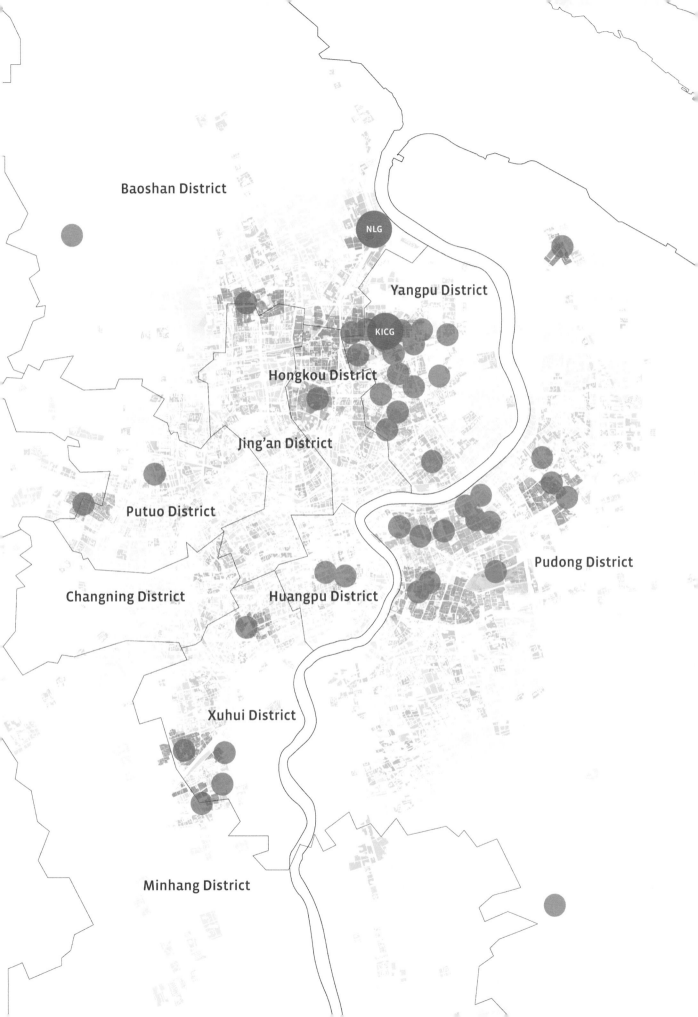

Baoshan District

NLG

Yangpu District

KICG

Hongkou District

Jing'an District

Putuo District

Changning District

Huangpu District

Pudong District

Xuhui District

Minhang District

60 Community Gardens, Yangpu District

Identify

May Garden Transformation – site in its original state: barren sealed space next to a community facility, enclosed between high walls.
The walls were taken down, the hard surface removed, and raised planting beds installed.

Rebuild

May Garden Experience – a green community space, based on permaculture principles from ecological planting to rainwater harvesting and composting, showcasing ecological processes for children to discover and learn.

Maintain

Elderly Volunteer Teams – having grown up in the countryside prior to China's industrialisation, community elders carry an abundance of knowledge about farming and enjoy sharing it with each other and the next generations.

A Place to Meet

Baicao Community Garden – one of the early community gardens built and maintained by residents. The 200 sqm garden is part of a pocket park and encompasses herb and flower gardens, fruit trees, and a composting area.

A Place to Discuss

Baicao Open Forum – a neighbourhood forum organised by Clover Nature School in the park. Urban gardeners can share their thoughts and discuss future measures and activities to ensure the success of the gardens.

A Place to Enjoy

Baicao Community – two primary user groups tend the garden: community elders and a volunteer gardening team of 24 children. Together, they organise activities such as the Lantern Contest at the Mid-Autumn Festival.

Self-seeding Gardens
Shanghai, Pudong District

Funding: Puxing Road District Council   Size: varies
Type: training, outreach programme   Year: since 2017

Approach Clover Nature School's community engagement programme follows a three-step approach, from managed learning and community centres to community gardens in co-governance and outreach programmes inciting self-governance. Over the years, the outreach programmes have taken on an increasingly vital role in Clover Nature School's mission and philosophy. Small groups or urban gardeners, trained by Clover Nature School and inspired by the community gardens of Yangpu district, are setting up gardens across Shanghai. As multipliers of the mission they start to change the urban fabric of the city through grassroots initiatives, gradually building up an ever-denser network of ecological stepping stones between the districts. Today, a total of over 300 community gardens at various scales and urban locations exist in Shanghai, and Clover Nature School aims even higher with a target of "2040 in 2040", as Liu Yuelai states with visionary foresight.

Programme With the ongoing development of co-governance community gardens in Yangpu district, word spread across the city. District representatives, neighbourhood groups, and private residents became interested in greening their local area. To meet the growing demand, Clover Nature School developed a set of training programmes to enable local communities to self-initiate ecological urban farming and gardening projects. The training workshop, in collaboration with Puxing Road residential district, is a fine example of this approach. In December 2017, twenty representatives of neighbourhood committees and residents from Puxing Road housing estates attended a workshop at Clover Nature School.
The certified five-day permaculture training course combines seminars and literature studies at the Knowledge & Innovation Community Garden (KICG) with guided practice modules and visits to the Nature Line Garden and the Yangpu district community gardens.

The first section of the training focuses on the fundamentals of sustainable urban farming and gardening. Participants are introduced to the concept of community gardens from a local as well as an international perspective. The methodology and best-practice examples of urban permaculture are shared in course materials and lectures. The morning classes are followed by site visits and practice of permaculture cultivation essentials in the afternoon, including sheet mulch cultivation, plant trimming, rainwater harvesting and ecological composting methods. Roundtable dialogues, during which the participants discuss the learning outcomes, and a practice workshop round up the sessions. During the practice workshop, miniature 'Carry-home Gardens' are created by each participant, allowing them to test their newly acquired knowledge and freely explore their own design ambitions.
The second part of the course is designated to knowledge building on plant selection and garden planning. The 24 Common Plants Atlas, an ecological gardening manual for community gardeners in Shanghai collocated by Clover Nature School, is handed out to participants to inform subsequent learning and practice. During the group visits to the Yangpu community gardens, participants are given the opportunity to directly raise questions and learn first-hand from the experience of the district's community gardeners. Manpower and enthusiasm are shared, and initial practical knowledge is applied to selected maintenance tasks. On the final day of the course, the participants gather one last time at KICG to evaluate the training and receive their certificates as urban gardeners.
After the training, the participants formed groups with like-minded gardeners to put into effect in their neighbourhood what they learned and practised during the five-day permaculture course. To date, over a hundred gardens have been created in Pudong district and numbers are growing.

Urban gardening training at KICG's Learning Centre ››

285 Community Gardeners, Pudong District

Spread

Self-seeding – community gardens at Puxing Road neighbourhood in Pudong district.
As a result of the training programme, 285 community gardens have been established and numbers are growing.

Training

Permaculture Learning Classes – group session on planting knowledge at the KICG Learning Centre. 24 Common Plants Atlas introducing Shanghai's most common plant species and their respective ecological value.

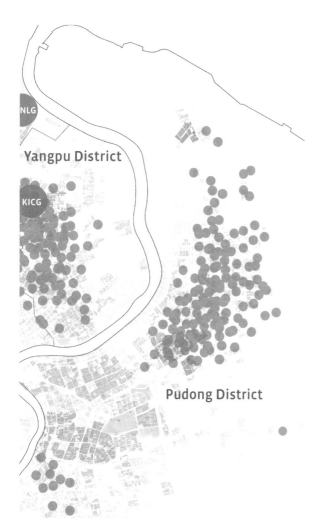

NLG

Yangpu District

KICG

Pudong District

Testing

'Carry-home Gardens' – workshop session: encouraging participants to test and apply the newly gained knowledge in miniature gardens and to freely explore and develop their own design aspirations.

Practising

Hands-on practice – participants visiting established community gardens and learning from first-hand knowledge. From corner gardens to small pocket parks, urban gardeners are joining forces for a greener Shanghai.

Certificate

Urban Gardener Certificate – after the training each participant is awarded a permaculture course certificate, on top of new friendships and network ties with like-minded urban gardeners in the community.

Guerilla Tulips
Shanghai, all districts

Funding: Shanghai Consulate General of the Netherlands, Shanghai Urban Planning Exhibition Centre, 2017–2018

Approach Every change begins with awareness. Initiated by Liz Christy and the original 'band of green guerrillas' in 1973, the community garden movement in New York City began as a grassroots response to the omnipresent decay in the city at that time. During their early 'seed green-aids' actions, the group threw seeds over fences of vacant lots, planted sunflower seeds in the medians of busy New York streets and placed flower boxes on window ledges of abandoned buildings, spontaneously greening the city and sparking public debate. Soon, the band turned their attention away from happenings to the ecological renewal of a vacant lot and created the Bowery Houston Farm and Garden, the first of over 600 community gardens in New York City today.

In 2017, Clover had the opportunity to collaborate with the Consulate General of the Netherlands on a charity event to 'Brighten up the City', by planting tulips across Shanghai: the Guerrilla Tulips, in reminiscence of the early guerrilla gardeners of New York.

Programme The Dutch Consulate each year gifts 4000 tulip bulbs to the city of Shanghai. Usually seeded as mass planting in public parks, in 2017 the consulate, together with Clover Nature School, employed a different approach, fostering direct public engagement. The 'Shanghai Citizen Growth Action' kicked off with a ceremony with speakers from the Dutch Consulate, the Shanghai Urban Planning Exhibition Hall, the Children Natural Experience Service, the Public Affairs Department of Shanghai Municipal Planning, and the Land and Resources Administration. The first thousand tulips were planted at KICG and Yangpu Community Gardens during the event, and fifty seedlings each handed out to dozens of community and school representatives. In addition, the citizens of Shanghai were invited to pick up tulip bulbs at various locations in the vicinity of KICG. In total, the 4000 tulip bulbs were planted in over thirty city boroughs.

As Clover Nature School describes their mission: "We want to encourage everyone living in the city to start paying attention to public space and let every corner of the block carry its stories." In spring, ten photos from the five hundred tulip fields recorded by residents were selected and 2000 postcards printed to preserve the memory of the grassroots colouring of the city.

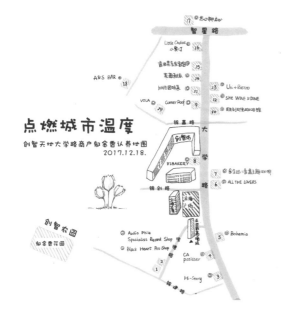

234

Tulip bulb pick-up locations ⌃

Guerrilla tulip blossom across town ››

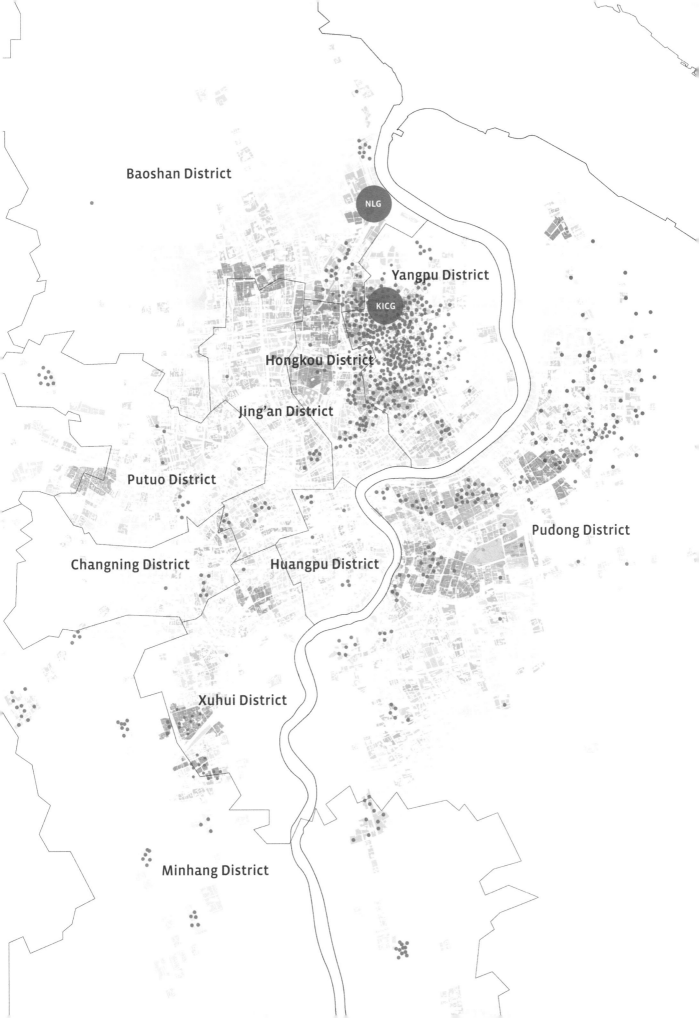

Baoshan District

NLG

Yangpu District

KICG

Hongkou District

Jing'an District

Putuo District

Pudong District

Changning District

Huangpu District

Xuhui District

Minhang District

4,000 Tulips, across Shanghai

'Brighten up the City' – a grassroots event to colour the city

"We want to encourage everyone living in the city to start paying attention to public space and let every corner of the block carry its stories."

Instinct Fabrication

Interactive Places

Beijing

Shenzhen

San Francisco

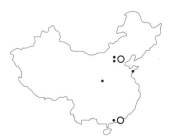

Instinct Fabrication

Beijing, Shenzhen, San Francisco

Founder: Lou Ying, Qiu Yu, Wang Zhujun
Founded: 2015
Team: 20–45
Location: Beijing, Shenzhen; San Francisco, United States
Portfolio: public parks, plazas, streetscapes, interactive landscape design, campus design, mixed-use commercial and residential design

Instinct Fabrication (IF) is an experimental landscape studio with twin studios in Beijing and Shenzhen. Founded in 2011 by Lou Ying, Qiu Yu and Wang Zhujun, the leadership team expanded in 2017 with Song Yingjia joining as Managing Director. The name of the studio reveals the programmatic synthesis of IF's design philosophy: a hybrid of 'Instinct' and 'Fabrication'. 'Instinct' refers to the inner logic of each project, whether it is concrete or experimental in nature. This fundamental key, the designers believe, is non-subjective and an essential prerequisite for addressing each project's core factually and appositely, unobscured by any notion of design, taste or fashion. Once that inner logic is untangled and defined, the process of 'Fabrication' begins, crafting and customising the design to represent the 'Instinct' of the project in the most appropriate, sleek and feasible manner.

The portfolio of IF spans from public urban spaces to residential landscapes and campus design. User experience and the application of new technologies are the trademark of IF's design across all landscape typologies. In their projects, the IF team strives for placemaking that activates the urban realm and encourages users to actively engage with their environment. With a proactive attitude towards design, IF creates places that address the rising demand from Chinese urbanites for a refreshed and user-centred way of public space design.

In conversation with Lou Ying, Wang Zhujun and Qiu Yu about studio culture, smart technologies in sustainable design and inclusiveness.

You all worked at leading international design companies in China prior to founding IF. What made you start your own practice together?

Lou Ying More than anything we are long-term friends. Qiu Yu and I met at Beijing Forestry University, where we both studied for our bachelor's degree. Zhujun and I met during our postgraduate studies in the US. Afterwards, we went our separate ways but always stayed connected.

Wang Zhujun Back in China, we all worked at large-scale international design firms. There were no small companies at that time. The market was basically divided between large-scale Local Design Institutes (LDIs)

Lou Ying is the Co-founder and Director of Instinct Fabrication. He oversees the portfolio and strategic development of Instinct Fabrication across all studios. In his creative work, he is particularly interested in addressing urban rituals and active engagement through public space design. Prior to founding Instinct Fabrication, Lou Ying worked at EDAW, San Francisco and AECOM, Beijing. He holds a Master of Landscape Architecture from Louisiana State University, Baton Rouge, Louisiana. Lou Ying is a member of the American Society of Landscape Architects and a visiting lecturer at Peking University

Qiu Yu is the Co-founder of Instinct Fabrication and Director of the Shenzhen studio. He directs the South China Region project portfolio of Instinct Fabrication and oversees the construction design and implementation of the projects across all studios. Prior to founding Instinct Fabrication, Qiu Yu worked at AECOM, Shenzhen and CRland Property Development, Shenzhen. He holds a Bachelor in Urban Planning from Beijing Forestry University.

Wang Zhujun is the Co-founder of Instinct Fabrication and Design Director of the Shenzhen studio. He leads the ecological and environmental studies of Instinct Fabrication and is the brain behind Instinct Fabrication's research and innovation in smart technologies and sustainable design. Prior to founding Instinct Fabrication, Wang Zhujun worked at Ecoland, Beijing. He holds a Master of Landscape Architecture from Louisiana State University, Baton Rouge, Louisiana, and a Bachelor in Environmental Studies from Chongqing University.

Song Yingjia is the Managing Director of Instinct Fabrication. Prior to joining Instinct Fabrication, Song Yingjia worked at Tsinghua Tonghen Planning and Design Institute, Beijing. She holds a Bachelor in Urban Planning from Beijing Forestry University.

<< Vanke Times Boulevard – acrylic mobile

Qiu Yu, Song Yingjia, Lou Ying, Wang Zhujun (left to right) – Instinct Fabrication team >>

and international design and engineering firms. These firms all share a similar setup, which is quite common in the landscape field in China. There are usually separate teams: one for concept and schematic design and a different team for design development. On top of this, only LDIs are licensed to draft and sign constructions drawings. In your everyday work as a designer, this means that the original design ideas are passed on to another team for design development and then again for construction drawings. There is no smooth process from design intent to the built result. The process itself makes it almost impossible to keep the design integrity from beginning to end. I guess we all shared this frustration.

Lou Ying Yes, and there is also another internal separation: the one between project management and design. As a designer, even at associate level, you hardly ever knew the whole picture. Projects looked promising, but then they were stopped. Sure, there were reasons. But now running our own design studio, we can make these risk assessments by ourselves. I personally think that is really important. Some projects may not have appropriate budgets or are not even profitable, but there are other things to gain, such as the opportunity to pursue an interesting design approach or a new type of project. Sometimes you have to take a risk because it can pay off in the most unexpected ways.

Sometimes you have to take a risk because it can pay off in the most unexpected ways.

Qiu Yu I went even a step further than Ying and Zhujun and moved on from design to design management on the client side. Most landscape projects in China are commissioned and managed by real estate developers. I wanted to gain the full picture, the entire perspective of the industry, also from within a developer company. Real estate companies in China often take on the role of project coordinators for large developments. They have various departments ranging from marketing, finance and sales to design, procurement and project coordination. As a design studio we need to face all these different departments, as they will comment at each stage of our design. But most of them aren't designers themselves. They come from very different backgrounds and areas of expertise. Having worked at a real estate company helps me better understand their comments and concerns – 'their language' you could say – and to decipher the 'brief behind the brief'. The smoother the communication, the smoother the process, and the greater the chance to achieve a design which works for both the client and future users.

The year 2014, when we started, was a special moment – a window of opportunity for small companies such as ours. The market was finally ready for small studios.

Lou Ying It is no coincidence, I believe. The year 2014, when we started, was a special moment – a window of opportunity for small companies such as ours. The market was finally ready for small studios. The economy was slowing down, projects were broken up into more phases and commissioned in smaller portions. Furthermore, developers were looking for fresh ideas and new companies, which could react more flexibly and quickly. Our office hierarchy is quite flat. All three of us are Directors and Design Principals at the same time. We can respond faster than large design companies. Chinese developers favour speed over all else.

Wang Zhujun What clients appreciate about us is that we really invest in making things work. There is a lot of 'talking' about sustainable design and creative ideas out there, but the real challenge is to turn those ideas into reality and ensure they can be built and function in the long run.

Lou Ying It is in our name. 'Instinct' and 'Fabrication' – understanding the 'nature' of the site and developing a suitable new 'skin'. We cannot change the world, but we can do our personal best to make it a better and more sustainable place.

It is in our name. 'Instinct' and 'Fabrication' – understanding the 'nature' of the site and developing a suitable new 'skin'.

Could you provide an example from your recent work of a 'sustainable and better place'?

Lou Ying G-Park is a good example of a prototype environment we created to involve visitors more actively in park life. So far Beijingers perceive city parks as places to breathe fresh air and enjoy the abundance of green. This is how they know parks from the past and hence what they expect. They are not aware of what else a park could offer.
We believe a park should be more than simply 'picturesque'. There are other values, such as health, for example. In G-Park, we wanted to surprise people and 'make them move' and become healthier by daring to jump and play. That especially applies for the young crowd in Haidian district. It is a university district. People there are young and energetic, but 'play-scapes' for young adults just don't exist. Physical activities in parks seem to be 'reserved' for children's play and elderly fitness only. In G-Park, we

combined smart technologies and young adult play by integrating reactive panels in the park pavement. When people stroll through the park now, they by chance may activate a water feature or mist spouts on the lawn. At first, they might be surprised by the chance encounter. But if they like it, they may tell others or come back with friends to play; perhaps start a jumping contest and share the moment on social media. In China, people like to gather and share things in a group. Small groups become bigger, creating a trend or an event. In G-Park, we also display the energy generated in the park by either the people or the smart technology devices on a LED screen in the park. You never know: the next generation of park users might start a game in how much energy one can generate. It is completely open for us. It is an experiment, a first impulse for people to start thinking about what they can do in a park and what a park could be.

Wang Zhujun We apply sustainable design methods in all our projects, not only at G-Park. What is new in G-Park is that we made the sustainable system 'legible' to the users. The LED screen is connected to a device which calculates and displays the 'sustainable figures' of the park in real-time, such as air quality, water storage, energy generation and consumption. Now park users can see what is usually hidden in maintenance protocols and understand more about sustainable design and living. We also use thin-film solar technology for additional energy harvesting. It is never perfect, but on a sunny day the solar lights and films can generate up to ninety per cent of the park's energy usage at night. All paving is permeable, and all stormwater collected in a dry well under the lawn. Beijing has a very dry climate and it hardly rains all year round. So, we won't ever be able to collect sufficient water for irrigation. But that only makes it even more important to harvest and store the limited natural water resources available in the most efficient way possible.

Both IF's ambitions and the spectrum of smart technologies applied at G-Park are quite daring. How did you gain the client's acceptance?

Lou Ying Well, that is the amazing part of working in China. Our clients are often more daring and visionary than us. Our idealism is in some ways constrained by buildability concerns. But clients have their brains wide open. They want new things and innovation. For G-Park, the owner actually approached us with the idea in mind of utilising smart technologies

It is an experiment, a first impulse for people to start thinking about what they can do in a park and what a park could be.

Well, that is the amazing part of working in China. Our clients are often more daring and visionary than us. Our idealism is in some ways constrained by buildability concerns. But clients have their brains wide open. They want new things and innovation.

Sunken plaza at the Beijing Global Financial Centre – work in progress – reinforced glass fibre planters and natural stone paving ‸

in the park. The site is located in a high-tech district. So, this made perfect sense to them – no need for us to convince anyone, only to prove that it can really work and how.

IF's projects often combine classic and 'smart' landscape materials. What role does materiality play in your projects?

Lou Ying I wouldn't make the distinction between new technologies and traditional landscape materials. The materials we use are a means, but not the objective of our design. In the end, all that matters is the user experience. Take Vanke Boulevard for example. The neighbourhood consists of mostly older estates dating from the 1990s, and the local community represents a mix of migrants from all different regions in China at that time. Our task was to restore the public realm. We reused all the paving on site. Sure, for budget concerns, but there is also another reason which is even more important. Let's call it inclusiveness through 'realness' in design. There is something very 'real' about these older estates. It is the ease with which people from different streams of life mingle there which fascinated us – and I believe this is also reflected in the materials on site. Instead of replacing the old granite pavers, we used a stone-flaming process to clean the original stones. No expensive new paving, no high-end finishes or the like – just a simple, good-quality material. I think simple is always good. It makes people feel comfortable. Everyone can grasp and appreciate simple and good quality. I remember the image of the construction workers, pausing at Vanke Boulevard and squatting at the timber deck we selected for this book. I like this photo a lot. For me, it captures our aim in one image: a well-designed landscape that is simple, inviting and open to all.

Qiu Yu We always strive for good construction quality and lasting materials. But our aim is beyond materiality. In our campus projects, for example, there are basically two main aspects which drive the design: the changing market demands and our personal observations. Education has always been high on the agenda in China, but campus design has just lately become a vital topic in landscape and architecture design. I think it reflects a shift in society. In the past, parents and teachers alike paid most attention to high scores and exams. But this attitude is changing. Today, parents are rather focused on the personal development of their

Inclusiveness through 'realness' in design – I think simple is always good. It makes people feel comfortable. Everyone can grasp and appreciate simple and good quality.

children. They want schools to enable children to develop their own character and direction in life. That is why school environments overall and outdoor spaces in particular are becoming increasingly important. In our campus designs, we create spaces for pupils and parents alike. In one of our projects in Shenzhen, for example, all the buildings are covered with green roofs. The children have their own organic farming lots there, and the parents and teachers can meet in open pavilions next to the fields. Another important aim of our campus designs is to maximise the freedom of play. We all have children and share similar observations.

In our campus design, we provide space for the children and a little challenge and some colour or surprise, and let them release their natural spirit of play.

Lou Ying Like my son, he doesn't like to play at setup facilities at all. He much prefers to create his own play, like balancing on a kerb and jumping from it. He uses every level drop in the city, or colour or whatever else might interest him. That is play for him. In our campus design, we provide space for the children and a little challenge and some colour or surprise, and let them release their natural spirit of play.

Compared to 2014, when IF started, how would you describe the landscape industry now? Where do you see the biggest change?

Lou Ying China is always changing, and fast. There are many more young landscape studios now. The competition has gotten fiercer, which I think is a good thing, as it pushes the general design quality of the industry to another level. The network of designers and our dialogue and exchange has become much stronger as well, as we are far more interlinked than compared to the years before WeChat.

Interestingly, you see WeChat as a crucial accelerator of change within the landscape industry in the past years. Why is that?

China is a vast country and real-time speed is important – also in communication.

Lou Ying Speaking about communication and networks, it is a different world now. Before we had to use email, which is never immediate. But with WeChat, everything is instant. It has not only changed the pace of communication, but also brought the industry closer together. It also reduced, if not replaced, the use of official online platforms, as we can directly post and share our projects with a wide audience at any stage of the design process from construction to final result. China is a vast country and real-time speed is important – also in communication.

Golden Riverside Patio

Foshan, Guangdong Province

Client: China Vanke Co. Ltd.
Type: residential, clubhouse courtyard

Size: 4,350 m²
Year: 2018

Place Golden Riverside is a high-end residential development in Foshan, a prefecture-level city with an urban population of 7.2 million located at the western valley of the Pearl River Delta Economic Zone. The patio is the centrepiece of the first phase of the new compound and will serve as a central community garden in the later stages of the project.

Approach Life in Chinese cities can be fast-paced, intense and exhausting at times – a continuous burst of sounds, images and information. With this in mind, IF opted for a patio design as a refuge from the city: creating a place of visual simplicity and a quiet antipode to the frenzy of the world around. Rooted in the notion that people not only perceive landscape design visually but are also affected by it on a psychological level, the designers envisaged a place that slows people down, encourages community and exploration, and above all provides a sense of relaxation and being welcomed at home.

Design The project design is based on three key objectives: easy circulation, a simplified landscape colour palette, and maximum freedom of inhabitation.
A covered walkway surrounds the garden patio as the main pedestrian access route. The courtyard-facing pillars of the walkway are eliminated in the design in favour of a single-sided cantilevered roof structure, permitting unobstructed views towards the central garden and pond. Five spherical planting beds with integrated mist and rhododendron cover shape the inner green. The garden paths meander between the planting mounts. They slow the pace of the visitors and increase their awareness of the surroundings. The central contemplation pond adds to this experience of aroma, art and mist. Dark slate tiles enhance the reflection of the pool and set the stage for the three drop-shaped fibreglass sculptures seemingly floating above the water.

The overall colour palette of the patio design is reduced to a minimalist juxtaposition of natural greens and pure white. All steel and concrete structures show a unifying surface white. While white represents a stage of purity and clarity, the textured greens calm the mind and encourage relaxation. Other than that, few colours are used and as spotlights only. Mist and mirror effects underline the ephemeral atmosphere of the garden, evoking a sense of strata and infinity.

Creating spaces for social interaction is key to community placemaking. The design of the communal areas of the patio is inspired by the local history of Foshan, as one of the four 'Cities of Assembly'. The characterisation of City of Assembly refers to the main regional economic hubs for business and trade in ancient times, where exchange and chatter was paramount in daily life and a quintessential means for the city to thrive. In alignment with this historic connotation, IF developed a four-arc bench. The benches are spaced yet face each other and allow for each single person's retreat as well as social interactions between neighbours, just as it happened centuries ago when Foshan was a vibrant centre of business and trade.

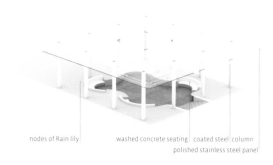

nodes of Rain lily   washed concrete seating   coated steel column
polished stainless steel panel

Central courtyard – mirror pavilion ››

Mirror pavilion – four-arc bench, reflecting roof ᴧ

248

‹ Central courtyard
– visual simplicity of
whites and greens ››

‹ Contemplation
pond and spherical
planting beds ››

‹ Waterdrop-shaped
floating sculptures
and entrance screen ››

‹ Four-arc bench,
flower nodes and
sweeping grass ››

Vanke Times Boulevard

Beijing, Chaoyang District

Client: China Vanke Co. Ltd.
Type: streetscape and plaza design
Size: 18,000 m²
Year: 2018

Place Vanke Times Boulevard is an urban rejuvenation project located in Wangjing, a subdistrict of Chaoyang district in the north-eastern metropolitan area of Beijing. The subdistrict is known as Koreatown and home to a dynamic blend of expatriates, primarily from South Korea, and Chinese migrants from across the country. Built in the late 1990s, the public realm of the neighbourhood shows a decay most prominent in Beijing's city expansion areas of that period. Poor pedestrian experience, outdated infrastructure, and a bland and barren appearance characterise these early residential estates today; a fact, which stands in striking contrast not only to the trendy new developments close by, but also to present-day demands on public space design. Currently pilot projects are being developed across China to tackle the pressing issue of the renewal of early city expansion areas. Vanke Times Boulevard, jointly led by Vanke property development and the district government, is one of the key initiatives researching inclusive and cost-efficient modes of public urban space renewal.

Approach Beijingers themselves, the designers of IF were stunned by the diversity of people and street life during their first visit to the site. Construction site workers, office employees, middle-class residents and delivery personnel all easily melded together and jointly inhabited the site: "It was so natural and instinctive that you could feel all were a real part of this place and will be a part of this renovation process in the future. Thus, we wanted to incorporate this sincerity and honesty into the design scheme, which envisions a cosy urban garden providing user-friendly amenities, embraces people from all walks of life who contribute to this neighbourhood, and safeguards their wellbeing through sustainable rectification to mitigate the hazards on site."

Design The site renovation follows the rule of: 25% Remain + 35% Refine + 40% Rebuild.

Remain: The terrace alongside the office buildings, ensuring access to all lobbies, remained unmodified.

Refine: At the plaza, as the main circulation concourse between the public realm and the underground retail areas, the existing pavement was removed, fire-flamed and reused on site.

Rebuild: The area along the perimeter of the site was restructured as a sequence of gardens, shielding the pedestrian areas from the adjacent parking lot.

As was common in Beijing's early mixed-use developments, the clearance between the finished floor level and substructure slab had been severely compromised, lacking space for underground piping and soil, and constraining the area to hard pavement without sufficient drainage, green cover and shade. IF reacted to this constraint by implementing a series of raised planters, introducing a green appearance and seasonal flowering palette to the site. Two spacious timber decks are integrated into the green buffer. Casual in nature, they offer a meeting place for all. A new passageway through the flowering grove completes the redesign of the perimeter zone. Drainage was another main concern for the refurbishment of the site. The newly implemented surface drainage system helped reduce the total site run-off by 45 per cent, keeping the area free of flooding during heavy summer rains for the first time since the completion of the estates.

Finally, an interactive sculpture at the entrance invites people to the gardens. Its vivid colours and playful nature are cherished by children and adults alike. It quickly became the signature element of the quarter and a wayfinding device for offices and restaurants nearby.

Bringing people back to the streets and uniting divergent lifestyles through landscape design is the primary success of this project. Furthermore, it establishes an exemplary case of landscape rejuvenation within restraint budgets, a model approach urgently needed for the ageing districts of Beijing's early city expansion.

Inclusive design – a casual meeting space for all ››

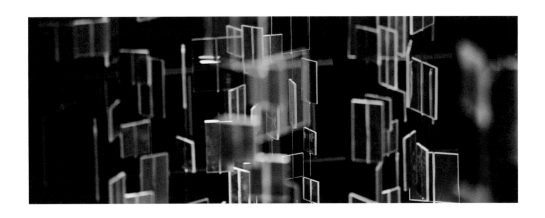

Greet: Acrylic mobile – children's play and wayfinding device ⌄

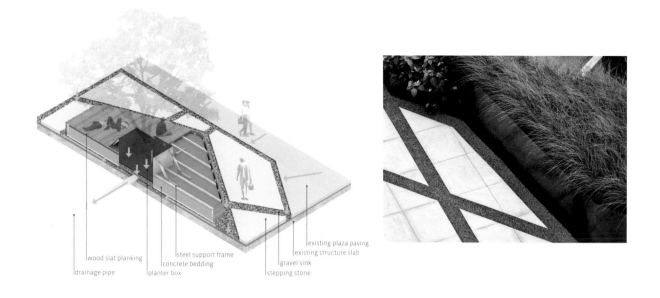

wood slat planking
drainage pipe
steel support frame
concrete bedding
planter box
existing plaza paving
existing structure slab
gravel sink
stepping stone

⌄ Refine: Garden sequence – raised planter beds and timber platforms, collecting stormwater run-off, greening the site

G-Park

Beijing, Haidian District

Client: Longfor Group Holdings Ltd.
Type: public park

Size: 5,000 m²
Year: 2018

Place The small pocket park is located in Haidian District, in the northern municipal area of Beijing. The district is home to leading Chinese universities including Peking University, Tsinghua University and Beijing Forestry University, alongside advanced technology companies including Huawei, Lenovo and Baidu. Both sectors equally contribute to and profit from the vibrant student culture and rich brain pool of the district.

Approach While Beijing has modernised and reinvented itself quite rapidly over the past decades, the same does not apply to the park system of the city. Traditional Chinese parks or recent adaptations still account for the majority of public parks in the city. With their related park programme leaning towards the picturesque and passive leisure, they fail to address current user demands and expectations of urban green. Thus, whilst there is no shortage in the numbers of public parks in Beijing, there remains a lack of qualified up-to-date park programmes able to attract young urbanites, from families to groups of friends or single city explorers alike. As IF states: "G-Park is a landscape experiment and design statement in favour of a refreshed look at urban park design and the recreational habits of its users. What if a park could generate the electricity needed for its maintenance and operations? What if a park could bring different people together to jointly activate the space? What if a park could increase the physical wellbeing of its visitors by engaging them in body movement?"

Design The design capitalises on the young urban spirit of the neighbourhood and the high-tech industries of Haidian district. A set of advanced technologies is applied on site, generating sustainable energy and water cycles. All smart devices are integrated into typical landscapes features, such as paving, structures, water features and irrigation systems, intentionally avoiding

any showcase effect of standalone high-tech products. Three main strategies structure the park programme and design: Firstly, the concept of body movement and interactive user experience is key to the park's design philosophy. This intent was made possible by a 'reactive panel' module, converting the intermittent pressure of moving weight from one point to another into electrical energy. Originally designed as an indoor utility device, the panel was tested and prototyped for outdoor use with the support of a high-tech solution consultant, and industrially manufactured after conducting a stable performance. The reactive panels are seamlessly integrated into the pavement of the park. When stepped upon, they trigger sprays of mist across the lawns and water jets inside the linear pool. Initially intended as a surprise effect, when walking through the park, the panels quickly became the park's main attraction, inciting visitors to jump and have fun in the park, whilst simultaneously generating clean energy to operate the water features. Energy harvesting is a second defining modus of the park. The concept was realised through thin-film solar technology and water storage devices. One resolves the energy cycle. The other collects, stores and reuses stormwater for irrigation purposes. Jointly, they establish a self-sustainable low-carbon water cycle for the park. 'Working-in-Nature' is the park's third main asset. An adaptable office cubicle composed of an iron steel frame and a glass panel façade serves as meeting room and workspace. With a simple switch of a button, the glass panels can be frosted, shifting the work atmosphere from open views to private mode.

G-Park is a projection into potential future models of a park. Since its opening, thousands of people have flocked to the small pocket park. Technology firms have visited and started looking into opportunities to strengthen ties between their laboratories and the landscape industry. To date, Haidian District is raising additional funding to extend the park.

Body movement – interactive water feature ››

Feel the force of nature penetrate your skin; Spin with ne tech.
as the magic sinks in.

Reactive panels – triggering clouds of mist across the lawns ∧

258

Minimalist dynamics >>

City of Legends
Qingdao, Shandong Province

Client: Longfor Group Holdings Ltd.
Type: public park, playground

Size: 20,000 m²
Year: 2018

Place Qingdao, also spelt Tsingtao, is a harbour city on China's northern coast. Looking out onto China's Yellow Sea, the city is home to one of the ten busiest container ports in the world and a major nodal city of the Belt & Road Initiative. The project by IF is part of a large-scale mixed-use commercial development in Jiaozhou, an upcoming district in western Qingdao. The new park forms the green arrival sequence to the City of Legends mixed-use development and mall, yet its design goes far beyond commercial space design by providing an active community space for the newly established residential quarters surrounding it.

Approach The design of the park is inspired by the idea of creating an 'X-space'. 'X' stands for unknowns in mathematics. In IF's design, it represents 'mystery and infinite possibilities'. The designers envisioned a park as a 'cross' of divergent spaces and atmospheres, increasing not only the connectivity of space but also the opportunities of chance encounters in space and time. The design integrates smart technologies, sports facilities and public art into a series of outdoor spaces encouraging community gatherings and interactive experiences within a landscape.

Design The sequence of outdoor areas starts at the High Plaza, followed by the High Park recreational fields and finally the High Wave bridge, which connects the park to the urban mall.
The High Plaza acts as the core feature area of the precinct. It consists of four elements: the morphing canopy structure, the digital water curtain, the interactive media floor and the colourful amphitheatre. Flexible in use, it caters for large groups at local events or festivals, as well as for daily visitors who come here to playfully engage with the dynamic media floor imagery or to quietly watch the ever-changing water display curtain.

Next in the spatial sequence of the 'cross' comes the High Park, or as the designers call it: 'the urban container of calories and energy'. Urban residents, seeking a healthier lifestyle, can partake in group sports or engage in casual physical activities here. Within a limited space, the High Park creates a modern, undetermined sports facility: visually strong and evocative, vibrant in colour and open to all user groups.
The last stop leads to the High Wave bridge. The pedestrian bridge spans 47 metres. It is designed as a journey, deciphering and depicting the rhythm of the stream of the water below and the pedestrian flow across. The handrail stands out as the core feature of the bridge design. No longer considered only as a mono-functional, linear safety element, the handrail becomes a multi-functional, three-dimensional object. Assembled out of nearly 600 single-shaped laser-cut steel tubes, the railing undulates vertically as well as horizontally: screening the views towards the canal and opening them in frames, widening for seating and retreating again, overall creating a winding journey across a linear element.
Since opening, the park has become one of the most frequented gathering spaces in the district, attracting people of all age groups and strengthening neighbourhood ties through unconditional encounters across the 'X'.

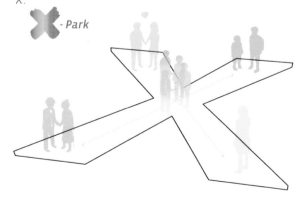

High Wave – undulating bench ››

'X' Park – a park of infinite encounters and possibilities ˄

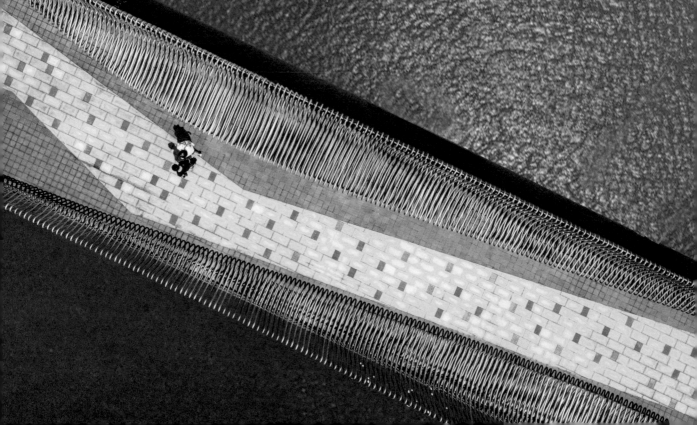

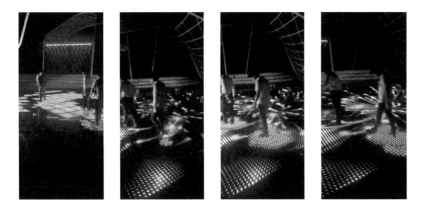

High Plaza – media floor testing ∧

Media floor – floating imagery triggered by people movement across reactive panels ∨

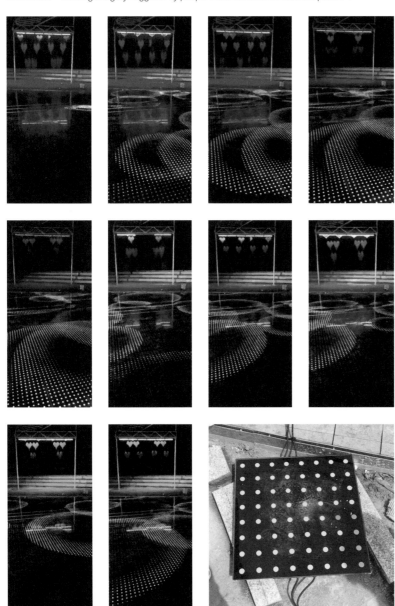

High Park –
'urban container of
calories and energy'

Leaders Primary School

Xi'an, Shaanxi Province

Client: China Vanke Co. Ltd.
Type: school campus design

Size: 19,500 m²
Year: 2019

Place Xi'an Leaders Primary School is a top-tier private school on the outskirts of Xi'an, a fast-developing metropolis in western China, known as the oldest of the Four Great Ancient Capitals of China. The school aims to set the highest standard in quality of education and progressive curriculum design as the leading educational establishment of STEAM (Science and Technology, interpreted through Engineering and the liberal Arts and based in Mathematics).

Approach As in previous campus projects by IF, the outdoor space design is determined by nature experience and an intricate blend of outdoor learning and play. Ample vegetation is embedded in all outdoor spaces, never as a singular element but always interwoven into the stair or plaza design. IF considers the integration of planting into campus design as a tool for the students to get in touch with nature, through direct experience of the texture, fragrance and materiality of plants and seasonal change. Touch; feel; know. Questioning the convention of buildings for learning versus outdoor spaces for play is the second thread in IF's design. Their campus design instead encourages learning through play and open-air classroom facilities.

Design The campus area is subdivided into three main activity courtyards and additional terrace areas designated to experimental farming and STEAM outdoor learning. The Amphitheatre Classroom in the west forms the largest courtyard. It receives sunlight for most of the day. A grand staircase with amphitheatre seating leads down to the main plaza of the compound. The flight of stairs is segmented by planting and work decks, offering a place for informal learning and casual group meetings and play. During lunchbreak, the plaza in front of the amphitheatre becomes the most popular space of the school, with students chasing each other and playing hide and seek.

In contrast to the open character of the spacious Amphitheatre Classroom, the second courtyard is far quieter and more secluded. Here, the mitigation of the 6.8-metre level drop of the terrain through varied modes of movement became the driver of the design, creating the Vertical Playground. Zig-zagging stairs, intersected by two colourful climbing ramps, stitch their way down the slope, next to a steel slide meandering through a steep ornamental grass carpet. By intertwining modes of level change from steps to ramps and slides, the courtyard became a three-dimensional playscape.

To the east, the third courtyard serves as the arrival square. Designed as a transitional plaza and waiting area for parents, the courtyard integrates arrival and farewell into the campus design philosophy. A semi-covered walkway connects all buildings of the compound. Alternating between openness and closure, multi-coloured resin panels cast a rainbow spectrum on the floor. Rainwater is collected for irrigation of the native planting, creating a small showcase biotope of experimental rooftop farming.

The small terrace next to the STEAM Learning Centre is dedicated to outdoor learning. Pupils can test and experiment with forces of gravity by playing with movable seating elements and a trampoline connected to a vacuum pump, converting the pressure generated by the children's movement into a display of flying balls.

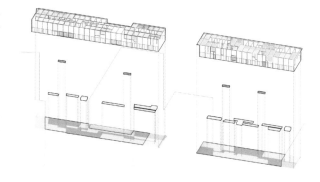

Vertical Playground and Rainbow Walkway ››

Rainbow Walkway – experimental roof garden ˄

existing levels
sunken courtyard

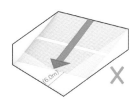

testing
regular stairs

step 1
zig-zag stairs

step 2
Vertical Playground

‹ Vertical Playground – modes of level change

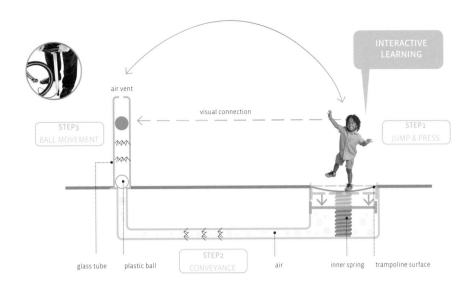

INTERACTIVE
LEARNING

air vent

STEP3
BALL MOVEMENT

visual connection

STEP1
JUMP & PRESS

glass tube   plastic ball   STEP2 CONVEYANCE   air   inner spring   trampoline surface

STEAM outdoor play – experimental learning ›

Amphitheatre Classroom – informal outdoor seating and work desks

Unconditional playscape – artificial topographies

lab D+H

Landscapes of Optimism

Shanghai

Shenzhen

Seoul

Los Angeles

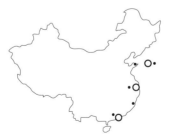

lab D+H
Shanghai, Shenzhen, Seoul, Los Angeles

Founder: Zhong Huicheng, YoungJoon Choi,
 Li Zhongwei
Founded: 2012
Team: 20–45
Location: Shanghai, Shenzhen; Seoul, South
Korea; Los Angeles, United States
Portfolio: public plazas, streetscapes, urban
renewal projects, playscapes and interactive
urban furniture design, artistic interventions

Lab D+H was founded in 2012 by Zhong Huicheng, YoungJoon Choi and Li Zhongwei. Originally based in Los Angeles, lab D+H has evolved into an international network studio with branch offices in Shanghai and Shenzhen, China and Seoul, South Korea. The work of lab D+H encompasses a wide range of project typologies and scales, ranging from commercial mixed-use and urban rejuvenation projects to public realm, playscapes, street furniture design and artistic site-interventions.

Lab D+H stands for 'laboratory of Design + Hope'. Designing places which carry a positive outlook on the future and can improve people's lives is at the core of lab D+H's design philosophy. It is this shared belief which unites the work of lab D+H across studios and projects, and which can be traced across projects at various typologies and scales. From artistic temporary landscape installations to colourful interactive streetscape design and carefully crafted urban renovation projects: all projects activate the urban realm, encourage the acknowledgement of the past and active participation in the future of the neighbourhoods. Lab D+H not only seeks to create places for people, but regards their designs as the missing link and incentive for the reconciliation of the divergent lifestyles engrained in the urban fabric of Chinese cities today.

In conversation with YoungJoon Choi, Zhong Huicheng and Li Zhongwei about optimism, micro-transformation, and craftsmanship and speed.

Lab D+H has a network structure with three studios at different geographies, each led by one of you as Creative Director. Looking back at the beginnings of lab D+H, what brought you together at first? How would you define your common ground and goals as a collective?

YoungJoon Choi We were actually discussing this topic recently prompted by an article I wrote. The essay was all about how we met and how we started our practice. It was titled: An Optimistic Generation of Landscape Architects. For me, that title sums up our primary design roots and drive.

So, optimism is the origin and spirit behind your work?

YoungJoon Choi Yes, if I were to condense it into one word, I would say

Zhong Huicheng is Managing Partner of lab D+H and the Creative Director of the Shenzhen studio. He ensures that each project of lab D+H opens up new possibilities for creativity and social responsibility. Prior to founding lab D+H, Zhong Huicheng worked at SWA Group, Los Angeles. He is a member of ASLA (American Society of Landscape Architects). Zhong Huicheng received his Master of Landscape Architecture with honours from Cornell University, Ithaca, and a Master of Engineering in Urban Planning from Beijing Forestry University.

YoungJoon Choi is Managing Partner of lab D+H and the Creative Director of the Seoul studio. His creative work is characterised by his culturally sensitive approach to design, prominent in lab D+H projects in Korea as well as in China. YoungJoon Choi is a member of ASLA and a registered landscape architect in the United States. Prior to founding lab D+H, he worked at SWA Group, Los Angeles. YoungJoon Choi holds a Master of Landscape Architecture with honours from the University of Pennsylvania School of Design, and a Bachelor of Landscape Architecture from Seoul National University.

Li Zhongwei is Managing Partner of lab D+H and the Creative Director of the Shanghai studio. The focus of his work lies on micro-transformation processes of high-density urban neighbourhoods and the preservation of traditional crafts. Prior to joining lab D+H, Li Zhongwei worked at SWA Group, Los Angeles and Sausalito, Field Operations, New York and WEST 8, Rotterdam. Li Zhongwei is a member of ASLA. He holds a Master of Landscape Architecture from Tianjin University and a Master of Landscape Architecture with honours from the University of Pennsylvania.

<< Yongqing Fang – recycled roof tile water wall

Zhong Huicheng, YoungJoon Choi, Li Zhongwei
(left to right) – lab D+H team >>

optimism. I think there were three major influences we were all exposed to as an entire generation of young designers, for which we have to be thankful. First of all, there was an 'open source' atmosphere in design, which was new. In contemporary design practice knowledge is not a black box anymore or a 'frozen' theory. Everything is open and readily accessible. When we were freshmen, we still had to go to the campus library to search for books. Today, you can just flip your browser open and find anything, from projects to theory, that you might be interested in. Every corner of the globe is always just a click away.

The exposure of the design process was another key driver and gift to our generation. Look at James Corner, for example. All of his design processes and theories were so clear and accessible to all. Same with Bjarke Ingels at BIG, whose strongest strategy lies in showing every single step of the design in very clear and at the same time also very intriguing diagrams. It is fun – almost artistic. Everything accelerated during the past decade through the use of digital technology. Nowadays, digital design methods allow us to immediately test our designs, develop them directly on screen, change drawings easily and visualise initial ideas in renderings or even video clips. That has changed a lot in the design process and even in the design communication with the client, in my opinion.

The third driver was the market and the abundance of work and project opportunities at that time. That is actually also how we met. Zhongwei and I both studied at UPenn and later worked at SWA, where we met Huicheng and decided to start our own office together. Usually, when setting up your own firm, you need to invest a lot of time and resources into marketing and business development. But when we started, we were actually immediately flooded with projects from China. We never had to worry about project wins or forecast. That also made us very optimistic.

Your studio name is an acronym for laboratory of Design + Hope. What does 'design plus hope' mean to you?

Zhong Huicheng 'Plus hope' is an important thread in our designs. We consider 'hope' as both our source and ultimate goal. It is a driver rather than a concrete objective. It is an immanent but open question that pushes us forward, that lets us continuously test our designs and stimulates us to grow further. For now, I would say 'hope' is in any innovation and any good influence on the environment or society. It is in the things we value

If I were to condense it into one word, I would say optimism. I think there were three major influences we were all exposed to as an entire generation of young designers, for which we have to be thankful.

We consider 'hope' as both our source and ultimate goal. It is a driver rather than a concrete objective.

and want to share in our designs. It is both our 'hope' and a 'hope' we want to provide and share with the people using the spaces we create.

Li Zhongwei Through the years of practice, our direction becomes clearer and clearer. We cannot predict what the future will be like, but we sure 'hope' to create places that can better the lives of people.

Lab D+H started off with a studio in Los Angeles. What made you move to China? How do you look at the landscape design industry here?

China has two characters: one is the speed of production, the other is the inherent culture and richness in craftsmanship and natural resources.

YoungJoon Choi While working at SWA, we were involved in projects in the US, but also in China and the Middle East. The fascinating thing about the China projects was the short duration. They went so quickly. Even in big projects, you could see the first results after a year or less. From my point of view, China has two characters: one is the speed of production, the other is the inherent culture and richness in craftsmanship and natural resources. These are the two main, sometimes conflicting but overall really fascinating modes of designing in China.

Li Zhongwei I think quickness is a good thing for designers. In practice, it means that no one expects that all parts of a project will be constructed a hundred per cent correct and perfectly. The projects may initially have flaws, but they are built and in large numbers, which gives you ample opportunities as a young designer to review your work – the real built work, not only the drawings – and understand whether the general direction you are heading is right. The chance to learn from the concrete built result to improve the next, that is the good part of working in China. All projects materialise very quickly. In this respect, China is very real, not just a place of visions and studies which may or may not come true.

China is very real, not just a place of visions and studies which may or may not come true.

Zhong Huicheng We consider the speed in China as a given, a special condition and mode of working with all its inherent pluses and minuses. The interesting part is how we address this issue in our projects. In this respect, we are all quite different. Zhongwei often works in urban restoration projects with an abundance of detailed 'character' works. That makes poor detailing a major factor, he is 'fighting' all the time. The Shenzhen studio focuses on public realm projects. Our strategy is to rather 'outsmart' the issue of construction quality through modular design.

The Shanghai studio of lab D+H has been involved in various pioneering projects in urban regeneration and adaptive reuse in China. Where does this fascination for old quarters stem from?

Li Zhongwei It comes from my personal attachment to old city quarters, which stems from my childhood experience. When I was young, my family lived in an old downtown area in the north of China. Later, my grandparents' home was demolished to give way for urban renewal. I still hold many vivid images and good memories of the life in the small alleys and courtyards and the intense neighbourhood culture in the old town. My grandfather often collected bricks from ruins and turned them into water basins or planters. Almost everything was made from bricks, old and new. Through this experience, I have a strong connection to these quarters. Keeping the memory alive and bringing it back into our daily lives is important to me as a landscape architect. To me, it means closing the gap between history and present and connecting people with their roots.

YoungJoon Choi I totally agree. That is true cultural practice. It is all about preserving the collective memory.

Li Zhongwei Landscape Urbanism was a crucial topic during our studies at UPenn. I feel the urban fabric today is infected by a kind of 'urban disease', and I believe that landscape architecture can be a 'good medicine' to cure this 'urban disease'. Take the urban planning of the past decades in China, for instance. All the new cities and city expansions look similar – bland cityscapes, endless repetitions of standard housing units, no identity, no flair, no memories. They have lost their connection with life, both present and past. But in the old town areas within the cities, we still can experience this genuine atmosphere of dense urban life.

Most importantly, those old neighbourhoods are spread across the city in China, as the urban fabric grew around them. One can find them in the centre as well as in the outskirts of the city, small islets of former downtowns often right next to new developments. This interwovenness makes them even more interesting as an incubator for urban change. Another aspect is the building materials in these neighbourhoods. Most are made from natural materials and tiles. They might be weathered by now, but that makes them only even more beautiful and intriguing. They carry meaning and history. That is why we often reuse the existing materials on site.

Keeping the memory alive and bringing it back into our daily lives is important to me as a landscape architect. To me, it means closing the gap between history and present and connecting people with their roots.

The urban fabric today is infected by a kind of 'urban disease', and I believe that landscape architecture can be a 'good medicine' to cure this 'urban disease'.

276

Micro-regeneration at Yongqing Fang – alley life after renovation, interlace of old and new structures inviting visitors and locals alike ‸

Simply put, our mission is: Keep, keep, keep. Keep the materials, keep the structure and traditional layout and keep the mix of history and present.

Zhong Huicheng It is the young people we want to address in these regeneration projects. Often, when they come to those quarters, it is their first time. It is unknown territory to them. The collective memory Young-Joon just mentioned might be not part of their memory. But they can learn from the history of the site and become excited about the lifestyle in those old neighbourhoods, once that life is made tangible for them. Some might just take it as another new fashion item, but this doesn't matter. It is the idea of an intense and culturally rich urban life which we launch and a showcase of sensitive and minimal impact design – that may gradually extend and change the urban fabric of Chinese cities.

Speaking of the contrasting urban fabrics of Chinese cities today – you are also working on new mixed-use projects. What defines your approach to public space design in these new neighbourhoods?

YoungJoon Choi The common ground of all our projects is placemaking. I lead the Seoul studio, but most of our projects are in China as well. Our approach is very close to the Shanghai studio's, as craftsmanship and materiality are equally essential to us. Only we approach it differently. In response to the issues of speed and low construction quality in China, we take a strategic decision at the start of each project about where to invest our work and energy. Costing in landscape design is always based on hardscape, softscape and element design. Usually, we 'calibrate' the charts towards the landscape elements. You may call it 'follies'– something new we bring in that can make the whole space 'shine'. That could be a shelter or a water feature or an element as simple as a bench; often a colourful and always a well-designed and detailed custom-made element, that provides a focal point, invites interaction and breaks the uniformity of the surroundings. That's our fast-track strategy for China. In many respects, it is quite similar to the Shenzhen studio.

Zhong Huicheng The designs of the Shenzhen studio are based on a modular approach. In our projects, we play on the relationship between a module at a small scale and the structure of the space at large scale. By structure, I mean the organisational logic of the space. So instead of

It is the young people we want to address in these regeneration projects. It is the idea of an intense and culturally rich urban life which we launch and a showcase of sensitive and minimal impact design – that may gradually extend and change the urban fabric of Chinese cities.

focusing on the details, we put our efforts into the spatial layout. The organisation of the space and the arrangement of the modules are our design instruments to make the spaces rich and engaging. The modules, in contrast, are fairly plain and repetitive, as we simplify not only the design language but also the material palette. This simplification is important especially in low-cost projects when construction workers are often not well trained and skilled. The single modules are easy to comprehend, which makes our construction drawings always very legible for the builders. To give an example, Tetris Square in Guangzhou is based on a singular module system which is 500 by 500 millimetres. All paving is based on that formula and aligned within this basic grid. Even for the furniture, we only used two types of precast modules. But when we arrange them in the square, we can turn them into dozens of spatial organisations, which allow people to interact and use the modules based on their needs.

In what way do you see lab D+H evolving? What will be the next goals and challenges?

YoungJoon Choi I am interested in complex cultural projects. In our new projects, we address healing landscapes and therapy spaces, which is extremely interesting and a novel challenge in our work.

Zhong Huicheng I will continue exploring modular systems and public interaction. Also, I believe in the future there will be a shortage in the supply of natural materials in China such as stone paving, which tends to be overused today. That is not sustainable by any means. The future lies in resource-conserving design, which is simple, fun, engaging and inclusive.

Li Zhongwei The micro-transformation of dense urban neighbourhoods is my main concern. I will keep on studying and trying to solve the urban problems through landscape design and in a China-specific way.

YoungJoon Choi Continuing this line of thought and our earlier discussion about design 'plus hope'. At the end of the day, 'social responsibility' is the best definition of 'hope'. I think social issues are what the young generation is most concerned about – so let's follow the 'hope' and make it happen.

The future lies in resource-conserving design, which is simple, fun, engaging and inclusive.

Roof Sentiment

Seoul, South Korea

Client: MMCA, Hyundai Card
Type: temporary installation
Size: 55 m²
Year: 2015

Place Roof Sentiment by SoA Architects (Society of Architecture) was the winning entry in the annual Young Architects Program (YAP) in Seoul, South Korea, in 2015. Originally launched by the Museum of Modern Art, New York, at its PS1 venue in 1998, the Young Architects Program fosters young, emerging architectural talents by providing them with the opportunity to design and build their visions. The programme has since expanded into an international network. In 2014, the National Museum of Modern and Contemporary Art (MMAC) in Seoul joined the YAP initiative, hosting annual competitions and exhibitions in partnership with MoMA, New York, and Hyundai Card, Seoul.

Approach Roof Sentiment is an artwork that echoes questions on the sensibilities of the roof as an architectural archetype, as well as a proposal for the means of occupation of civic voids. The roof is made by plaiting, spreading and hanging reeds, a material traditionally used in Korean crafts. Roof Sentiment is not a mere roof covering a structure, but acts as a vessel that houses a scenery as well as a device to conjure the sensibilities of the visitors. This combination of a roof as a known means of shelter, and the ambiguity and reference to nature, prompted by materiality and shape, identifies the installation. It raises the visitors' awareness of cultural experiences and forgotten sensibilities in the midst of busy daily schedules.

Design After the competition stage, the architects of SoA collaborated with the landscape architects of lab D+H to advance the original proposal into a full scope courtyard design. Sharing the same mindset and beliefs, the designers of SoA and lab D+H jointly established a spatial setting encompassing ground, structure, roof, and sky united by a vernacular palette of materials and applications. In reference to traditional Asian garden art, the design of the museum courtyard is not approached as a civic plaza, configured by and serving the buildings around, but as a window to nature, borrowing the scenery from buildings and sky. When sourcing the material for the large-scale reed sheets of the pleated roof, lab D+H benefitted from its transnational network of studios. Not available at size in South Korea, the sheets were manufactured in Shandong province in China and shipped to Seoul.

To further evoke a sense of nature at ground level and to enrich the tactile experience of the users, the ground surface below the canvas is covered with shredded pine bark, suffusing the air with its scent. The selected plant collection belongs to the same botanical family as the fabric of the roof. Subtle landforms surround the waving folds of the roof, adding a topographical layer to the courtyard. The landforms conceal the base of the structural columns and soften the divide between the ground and the roof at experiential level. The tallest landform invites people to climb up and take a glimpse through the plaits. The mound is placed in alignment with the symbolic visual axis of the adjacent Gyeongbokgung Palace and Ingwan Mountain. Paving stones removed from the courtyard were reused for the paving of the entrance area. Broken pavers were recycled and became an impromptu land art installation throughout the pine bark floor.

Roof Sentiment is an artwork to awaken people's sentiment of the roof: shielding and exposing, covering and yet simultaneously uncovering people's sensations and sensory experiences.

Reed folds – topographies and perspectives ››

Traditional reed cutting ⌃

< Impromptu artwork of recycled stones

< Pine bark – natural scents

< Folds and topography

Roof Sentiment is an artwork to awaken people's sensibility of the roof, shielding and exposing, covering and yet simultaneously uncovering people's sensations and sensory experiences ››

Yongqing Fang

Guangzhou, Guangdong Province

Client: China Vanke Co. Ltd.
Type: urban renewal, public space design

Size: 30,000 m²
Year: 2017

Place Yongqing Fang is a traditional neighbourhood located in the heart of Guangzhou's old quarters. The southern metropolis, with an urban population of 13 million to date, has been the major economic centre of South China for centuries. In recent years, the city has seen a boom again, with a surge in urbanisation at the city fringe as well as in the inner-city quarters.

In 2014, Vanke Group spearheaded a major transformation process for the Old Town of Guangzhou. The renewal strategy established in close collaboration with local government bodies prioritises the preservation of the existing urban as well as social fabric above replacement and relocation, and aims to strengthen the commercial vitality of the local community through a balanced mix of living and working, and restored as well as new cultural facilities.

Approach The design of lab D+H for Yongqing Fang takes a stance in response to the rapid urban transformation of modern-day China, which tends to mono-programme urban quarters and segregate old from new, living from working and ultimately challenges the unity of the civic society. As lab D+H observes: "Transformation often pushes out old residents to make way for new ones. In this destructive process, the history and charm of the old neighbourhood is lost. Instead of perpetuating this cycle, we reimagine abandoned alleyways as unique spaces for both new and old residents to meet. After completion, Yongqing Fang quickly became a thriving cultural landmark again, with residents, tourists and entrepreneurs all coexisting harmoniously. By creating inclusive public spaces, cities break down social barriers, crafting a future where everyone feels they belong."

Design The architectural renewal of Yongqing Fang by Atelier cnS follows three basic categories, depending on the ownership and current state of the building structures: minimal modernisation and upgrade of safety fixtures where requested by the owners; refurbishment of mansions and traditional houses; and demolition of hazardous structures and replacement of dilapidated houses by new buildings. None of the new architectonic interventions aims to mimic the olden days. Restored heritage buildings next to traditional townhouses and brand-new apartments and workshops are lining the alleys after renovation, jointly creating a visual statement of transformation.

The landscape architecture design follows the same approach: old pedestrian alleys were restored and retrofitted; the two main squares were redesigned, combining modern aesthetics with traditional crafts; while the roof terraces of the new courtyard buildings show a casual contemporary interface. In the alleys, the original layout of raised, granite kerb blocks along the townhouses was kept intact. The large stone pavers were removed during construction and reinstalled after completion of the new subsurface drainage system and electrical wiring. The renewed kerb line has an added feature: recessed lighting provides a warm ambient light, gently illuminating the alleyways at night. The central area of the quarter is designed as two corresponding plazas: a small quiet sitting space next to a water wall and a public gathering area around a stage. In the side alleys, a third small plaza at the forecourt of Bruce Lee's ancestral home celebrates his famous quote of 'empty your mind, be formless, shapeless like water … be water, my friend' with a water sculpture.

Zero-waste design was key to the restoration process, material sourcing and construction. The tiles of all derelict roofs were collected and reused to create the water features at the squares. Staggered in response to weight and structure, the former roof tiles create the water wall at the main square. Previously hidden from sight, they now reveal their artistry and craft to passers-by, turning the old and preserved into a design statement of the new and thriving.

Alleyways – inclusive design – a portrait of old and new ››

Before renovation:
‹ Central square
‹ Alleyways

Central square and alleyways – refurbished traditional paving and kerb lines, signage, recessed lighting ⌄

Central stage ›

Zero-waste design:
‹ Dilapidated roofs
‹ Roof tile collection and reuse

Forecourt of Bruce Lee's ancestral home – *"empty your mind, be formless, shapeless like water ... be water, my friend."* ⌄

Roof tile water wall >

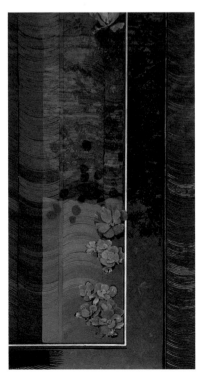

Yantai Mountain

Fuzhou, Fujian Province

Client: China Vanke Co. Ltd.
Type: restoration of alleyways and courtyards

Size: 18,750 m²
Year: 2019

Place During the nineteenth and early twentieth century, Fuzhou's concession area at Yantai Mountain was the city's landmark of prosperity. The silhouette of wealthy mansions and consular missions punctuated the hillside, rising above the busy trading ports of Mingjian River. In the 1841 Treaty of Nanking, signed by China and the United Kingdom after the First Opium War, Fuzhou was earmarked as one of the treaty ports, open to foreign trade. Yantai Mountain in particular became a centre of global trade in tea. With the founding of the People's Republic of China in 1949, Yantai Mountain lost its economic pre-eminence and gradually fell into decay. The former commissioners' mansions were reused for conventional purposes or left abandoned. The Nine Alleyways leading up the hillside, once busy merchant lanes, became derelict and forgotten.

With heritage conservation high on the national agenda in recent years, the hillside of Yantai Mountain regained the attention of local and provincial governments. In 2017, lab D+H was commissioned to restore the historic alleyways of Yantai Mountain and the courtyards of the remaining heritage buildings, including the forecourt and garden of the now-refurbished American Consulate mansion, a hallmark project of the restoration initiative, housing the Yantai Mountain Urban History Museum and the History & Culture Exhibition Hall.

Approach Faced with the rare task of rejuvenating a colonial-era site, the designers of lab D+H were most fascinated by the convergence of Western and Eastern influences, reminiscent in the architecture style and building structures but even more so in the outdoor spaces, in both the original state of the design as well as in the adaptations made in subsequent years. This fact became most evident during a comprehensive survey of historic documents, including early photos, drawings and county records. In addition, the designers conducted a series of interviews with local residents born between

1940 and 1980 and eyewitnesses to the changes on site. Consequently, the design of Yantai Mountain by lab D+H enjoys a blend of Western special features and Eastern local craftsmanship, materials and patterns. Alternating between restoration methods applied at the historic mansion yards and adaptive reconstruction throughout the public realm of the hill, the design preserves the past, where of historic significance, and injects new interpretations where contemporary life has moved in.

Design The outdoor areas of the Yantai Mountain Urban History Museum are designed in close reference to the formal layout of the historic gardens of the American Consulate in the late nineteenth century. Two 200-year-old camphor trees and four mature banyan trees are preserved. Yantai Mountain is known as the Dock of Plum Flowers, portrayed in the poems of Xu Tong during the Ming dynasty. In honour of his praise, the design incorporates plum flower motifs at the restored entrance gate, perimeter walls and water feature. In the public realm, the alignment of the historic Nine Alleyways was retained, and the stairs and pathways restored. Where intact, the original granite steps were kept, and gaps filled with custom-made replacement stones. The paving follows the same principle. Original granite pavers were collected on-site and reused in a mixed paving palette, together with new granite paving stones. The typology of rebuilt walls ranges from new contemporary brick stone walling to restored granite retaining walls and traditional decorative walling. The rebuilt walls along Tingxia Road are a fine example of this approach. Local craftsmen who had already retired were invited to join the restoration team and to share their knowledge of traditional tools and methods.

The redevelopment of Yantai Mountain thus not merely preserves the tangible heritage of the site enshrined in layout and material, but also its intangible legacy, captured in traditional crafts.

Yantai Mountain – concept drawing ››

∧ Mingjian River, 1890 – in its heyday, the district accommodated over 60 brokers, 30 foreign firms, 14 churches and dozens of missionary schools as well as consulates and agencies from over 17 foreign countries – including the United Kingdom, the United States, France and the Netherlands

MINJIANG RIVER

美豐銀行 MEIFENG BANK
羅宅 LUO'S HOUSE
洪宅 HONG'S HOUSE
煙台山公園 YANTAI MOUNTAIN PARK
樂群樓 LEQUN BUILDING
文苑 WEN GARDEN
閩海關稅務司 CUSTOMS TAX BUREAU
協和建築部 XIEHE BUILDING DEPARTMENT
石厝教堂 SHICUO CHURCH
法國領事館 FRENCH CONSULATE
槐蔭里四號 HUAYINLI NO.4
亭下路 TINGXIA ROAD
海軍宿舍 THE NAVY'S DORMITORY
盛興洋衣坊 SHENGXING TAILOR SHOP
美國領事館 AMERICAN CONSULATE

Nine Alleys

‹ State before renovation

‹ Heritage walls, weathered stairs

‹ Restoration prototyping

Nine Alleys – restored stairways and lanes ⌄

292

Brick stone works ›
Contemporary perimeter walls
Restored traditional walls

American Consulate
‹ Historic photograph – Mr Howard's House

Yantai Mountain Urban History Museum (former American Consulate) – water features depicting plum flowers ⌄

River terrace ›

Entrance courtyard ›

Birdcage pavilion ›

Bridge 3

Shanghai, Baoshan District

Client: Kicers Investment Holdings Ltd.
Type: adaptive reuse, public space design

Size: 25,000 m²
Year: 2019

Place Bridge 3 is the newest project of Kicers Group, previously known as Lifestyle Centre Group Limited. Founded in 2002, Kicers Group is dedicated to the integration of knowledge and capital to develop better living spaces for the new mainstream consumers in China. Bridge 8, Kicers Group's founding project, located in the EXPO Puxi Zone in Shanghai, was the first project in China to link urban renewal with the concept of a creative industrial park and instantly became a hallmark of adaptive reuse in Shanghai. Bridge 3 is one of the successor projects of the same line, rejuvenating the abandoned inner-city industrial site of Shanghai Nissho Vacuum Flask Refill Company into a neighbourhood commercial centre and community hub. Strategically located at the conjunction of Baoshan, Hongkou and Yangpu districts, Bridge 3 has become a true civic bridge between the districts.

Approach As with Yongqing Fang and Yantai Mountain, lab D+H's work at Bridge 3 is concerned with the preservation of memory. In contrast to the previous projects, at Bridge 3 lab D+H recognised remembrance as inherent to the space and scenes rather than the materials and patterns. The protection of the mature camphor trees on site and the conservation of the post-industrial character through the framing of essential scenes became the project's defining task.

Design At commencement stage, mature camphor trees still lined the alleyways of the deserted industrial site, their slender canopies far surpassing the factory buildings in height. Together with the chimneys of the factory, they form the site's defining silhouette, engrained in the mental map of the districts' residents. The protection of existing trees became the leading objective of the landscape design during site construction and a taxing task, as tree protection measures are new to China and still underregulated. With the exception of

the mature signature trees at the plaza, the designer succeeded in preserving all the trees along the alleyways and at the perimeter of the site. The majestic camphor trees now line the refurbished pedestrian lanes. They anchor the new design incisions in the site's history and mediate between new and old. Their canopies provide shade and shelter in the cool of the morning hours and throughout the heat of Shanghai's summer months. Raised planters with casual timber seating protect the base of the trees.

The new Civic Plaza stands out in the set of post-industrial scenes on site. Refurbished factory buildings surround the plaza. They serve as community centres for childcare and civic facilities. The design of the square is intentionally minimalist. Its appearance is strongest in the evening, when the city cools down and people flock into the streets. A grid of colourful floor lights, in combination with outdoor cinema projections on the perimeter wall, sets the stage for casual evening meetings and large-scale events against the backdrop of the illuminated chimney towering above the plaza.

The Health Line with linear play equipment and the Market Square below the skeleton of the stripped steel truss of the former factory roof complete the set of public spaces, which guide the visitors through a sequence of scenes uniting post-industrial frames with everyday life.

Evening scene – lighting grid and projections ››

Factory silhouette – chimneys and trees ⌃

‹ Lanes at construction stage

Refurbished pedestrian lanes – preserved camphor trees, raised planter beds, informal seating ⌄

Chimney passage ›

Pedestrian lane ›

Central plaza ›

Kunyu Mountain Rest

Yantai, Shandong Province

Client: Kunyu Mountain Park Management
Type: park amenities

Size: 250 m²
Year: 2018

Place Kunyu Mountain National Park is a scenic mountain area east of Yantai city, at the tip of Shandong peninsula, recognised as a nature reserve in 2008. In 2018, Kunyu Mountain Park Management undertook a series of amenities upgrades throughout the 50-square-kilometre national park and invited lab D+H to conduct a pilot study for new restroom facilities.

Approach With no location determined in the brief, lab D+H commenced the study by introducing a modular system of facilities, adjustable to different topographic conditions across the mountain range. This site-adaptive approach was greatly appreciated by the park management team and conjointly a site was selected to build the first prototype facility: a restroom at a terrace within the alpine botanical garden at the fringe of the forested hills.

The second thread of the design equally stems from the reinterpretation of the initial brief. Whilst the Chinese text simply called for a 'toilet', the American expression 'restroom' prompted a potentially much wider program description of the place, implying a place for resting. Thus, instead of designing an enclosed, boxed toilet service station, lab D+H opted to create an all-encompassing resting place in dialogue with its surroundings and in tribute to the sensitive nature of the place.

Design The general configuration of the new park amenity follows a courtyard setting. Modules of restroom facilities and additional open shelters jointly form a yard, seamlessly adapting to the existing contour lines. Short stairs and ramps connect the different modules across levels. A canopy of modular roofs surrounds the patio, providing shelter from the elements and enclosure where desirable. The diagonal layout of pitched roof units shapes the characteristic geometric silhouette of the facility in response to the outline of the rugged mountain ridge.

The service station is divided into two areas: the raised southern resting platform for people pausing and enjoying the mountain views, and the northern bathroom facilities, located away from views and immediate arrivals. The hand basins are combined at two service points at the fringe of the courtyard, where the greywater can be directly cleansed and discharged on-site. When assembled on-site, the iconic silhouette of the pitched roofs immediately revealed its potential as a signature feature of Kunyu National Park, a man-made nucleus carefully crafted against the vastness of the mountain range. In addition, the low-impact design through modular systems has proven to be a great asset for the amenity upgrade endeavour of Kunyu National Park: combining recognisability with variability in the scale and layout of the amenity programmes, and flexibility in location through a site-adaptive design strategy.

300

Modular design – creating openness and shelter ››

Geometric roof silhouette ⌃

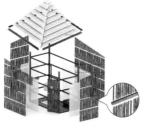 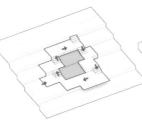 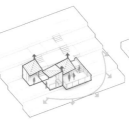 

CREATE COURTYARD AND LOOP   RAISE TO CREATE WELCOME STRUCTURE   RAISE TO CREATE RESTROOM STRUCTURE

Index

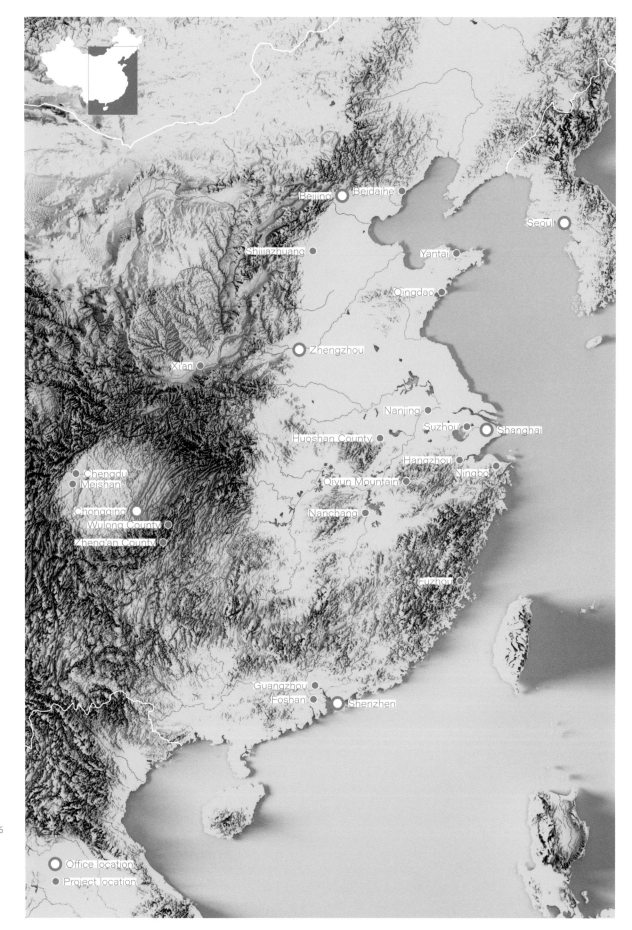

Beijing ○ ● Beidaihe

Seoul ○

Shijiazhuang ●

Yantai ●

Qingdao ●

Zhengzhou ○

Xi'an ●

Nanjing ●

Suzhou ● ○ Shanghai

Huoshan County ●

Hangzhou ●

Ningbo ●

Chengdu ●
Meishan ●

Qiyun Mountain ●

Chongqing ●
Wulong County ●
Zhengdan County ●

Nanchang ●

Fuzhou ●

Guangzhou ●
Foshan ●
○ Shenzhen

○ Office location
● Project location

Places | Projects

Beidaihe
Z+T Studio | Aranya Children's Farm

Beijing
IF | Vanke Times Boulevard
IF | G-Park

Chengdu
Z+T Studio | Cloud Paradise Park

Chongqing
WISTO | Longfor Island
WISTO | Studio Urban Farming

Foshan
IF | Golden Riverside Patio

Fuzhou
lab D+H | Yantai Mountain

Guangzhou
lab D+H | Yongqing Fang

Huoshan County
Fu Yingbin Studio | Rural Acupuncture

Hangzhou
Z+T Studio | Royal Territory

Meishan
WISTO | Canyon of Light

Nanchang
YIYU | AVIC Park
YIYU | Shower of Light

Nanjing
Z+T Studio | Tangshan Quarry Park

Ningbo
Z+T Studio | Jia Zhu Li

Qingdao
IF | City of Legends

Qiyun Mountain
WISTO | Freedom Tree House

Shanghai
YIYU | MOMA Museum Waterfront
YIYU | Silhouette Garden
Moshang | Elegant Mansion
Moshang | Rong Garden
Moshang | Royal Garden
Clover | Community Gardens
Clover | Guerilla Tulips
Clover | KIC Garden
Clover | Nature Line Garden
Clover | Self-seeding Gardens
lab D+H | Bridge 3

Shijiazhuang
Moshang | Violet Palace

Suzhou
Z+T Studio | The Park
Z+T Studio | Yue-Yuan Courtyard
YIYU | Gallery of Nature
Moshang | Lake Mansion
Moshang | Jinlin Cloud Mansion

Wulong County
WISTO | Village of Return

Xi'an
IF | Leaders Primary School

Yantai
lab D+H | Kunyu Mountain Rest

Zheng'an County
Fu Yingbin Studio | Zhongguan Village Renewal

Seoul, South Korea
lab D+H | Roof Sentiment

Contributors

 **Kristin Feireiss** is an Architecture Curator and the founder (together with Helga Retzer, † 1984) and Director of Aedes Architecture Forum in Berlin. Founded in 1980 as the first independent architecture gallery worldwide, Aedes's exhibitions and publications contribute to an extended understanding of architecture and urban design, including their cultural, social and economic factors. Kristin Feireiss was Director of the Netherlands Architecture Institute (NAI) (1996–2001) and Jury Member of the Pritzker Architecture Prize (2013–2017). She holds the Cross of Order of Merit of the Federal Republic of Germany and is a Knight in the Order of the Netherlands Lion.

 **Ron Henderson** is Professor and Director of the Landscape Architecture + Urbanism Program at the Illinois Institute of Technology (IIT) in Chicago. Previously, he was member of the founding faculty of the Landscape Architecture Department at Tsinghua University, Beijing (2005–2011). He is Senior Fellow of Garden and Landscape Studies at Dumbarton Oaks, Japan-US Friendship Commission Creative Artist Fellow, Fellow of the American Society of Landscape Architects and author of *The Gardens of Suzhou* (2012). He is Founding Principal of L+A Landscape Architecture, whose work includes the roof garden for the China Pavilion at the 2010 Shanghai Expo.

 **Claudia Westermann** is Senior Associate Professor at Xi'an Jiaotong-Liverpool University, Suzhou, China, and Lead of History, Theory and Heritage in the Department of Architecture and Design. With an academic background in both Architecture and Media Art, her practice and research engage the ecologies and poetics of art and architecture in the context of a technologically created present. Her works have been widely exhibited and presented, including at the Venice Biennale (Architecture), the Moscow International Film Festival, ISEA Symposium for the Electronic Arts in Japan, the Centre for Art and Media (ZKM), Germany and the 2019 Yanping Art Harvest in Fujian.

Jeffrey Hou is Professor of Landscape Architecture at the University of Washington (UW), Seattle. As Director of the Urban Commons Lab at UW, his work focuses on public space, democracy and civic engagement. He is recognised for his work on guerrilla urbanism and bottom-up placemaking, through collaborative publications including *Insurgent Public Space: Guerrilla Urbanism and the Remaking of Contemporary Cities* (2010), *Transcultural Cities: Border-Crossing and Placemaking* (2013), *Messy Urbanism: Understanding the "Other" Cities of Asia* (2016), and *Design as Democracy: Techniques for Creative Creativity* (2017).

Jutta Kehrer (ed.) is Director at LAC, Hong Kong. Previously, she was Head of Landscape at Antaeus Group, Beijing and Design Director at AECOM, Beijing. She is a regular contributor to Topos, International Journal of Landscape Architecture and Urban Design, on Asian design. In addition, she engages in academic teaching, including at the University of Stuttgart, Germany, the University of Tokyo, Japan, the University of New South Wales (UNSW), Australia, the Academy of Architecture Amsterdam, Netherlands and the University of Hong Kong (HKU) and Birmingham City University (BCU)/SHAPE, Hong Kong.

Acknowledgements

Above all, I would like to thank the founding principals of the studios featured here for their time and openness in support of this book, and the many inspiring insights, stories and debates shared at the various project sites, around tables of delicious food and in virtual sessions, when the pandemic struck and made us all pause on the spot.

In many ways, the making of this book was a journey in itself and wouldn't have been possible without the support of many others who contributed to the book along the way.

I would like to express my special thanks to Dorothy Tang and Maxime Decaudin, without whose critical review and encouragement during the early stages this book would not have come into being.

The editorial team who supported the publication from their various field of expertise has been an invaluable anchor point throughout all stages of the making. I am clearly indebted to Peng Li for her insights into Chinese culture, her interpretation beyond translation and her companionship throughout the months, both remotely and in-person during our travels. A special thanks goes to Maik Novotny whose critical reflections as an architectural writer from conception to content were equally indispensable. Moreover, I would like to thank Ido Vock for his rigour paired with curiosity when faced with editing an abundance of Chinese proverbs and terms, and Jiang Xinjie for her impeccable transcripts and translations.

Furthermore, I would like to thank all staff members of the studios involved in the collection and preparation of documents for this publication for their time and dedication. I would like to especially single out Cecilia Zhang, Huang Siqui, Ji Lin and Song Zikang: your contributions as communicators and organisers have been priceless.

Of the independent organisations that contributed to this book, I would like to especially thank Gao Kun and Deng Qiao for a wonderful day at Luxelakes, and the Special Collections team at the Cadbury Research Library for their exceptional efforts to confirm and grant image rights while the archives remained closed.

My thanks go to the editorial, production, sales and marketing teams at Birkhäuser without whom this book would not exist. But primarily I would like to offer my thanks to David Marold and Angelika Gaal for their confidence, support for and appreciation of this publication.

Lastly, my heartfelt gratitude goes to Angela Silbermann, Hee Sun Choi, Janette Watt and Petra Mager who critiqued and encouraged me throughout the journey of the making with their incisiveness and smiles.

Photo Credits

Colophon

Editor
Jutta Kehrer, Hong Kong

Acquisitions Editor
David Marold, Birkhäuser Verlag, Vienna

Content and Production Editor
Angelika Gaal, Birkhäuser Verlag, Vienna

Proofreading
Alun Brown, Vienna

Graphic design
www.doppelpunkt.com

Printing
Holzhausen, die Buchmarke der Gerin Druck GmbH, Wolkersdorf

A CIP catalogue record for this book is available from the Library of Congress, Washington D.C., USA
Library of Congress Control Number: 2020943215

Bibliographic information published by the German National Library
The German National Library lists this publication in the Deutsche Nationalbibliografie; detailed bibliographic
data are available on the Internet at http://dnb.d-nb.de

ISBN 978-3-0356-2145-7
e-ISBN (PDF) 978-3-0356-2149-5

Printed in Austria

© 2020 Birkhäuser Verlag GmbH, Basel
P.O. Box 44, 4009 Basel, Switzerland
Part of Walter de Gruyter GmbH, Berlin/Boston

9 8 7 6 5 4 3 2 1
www.birkhauser.com